1 My Desk

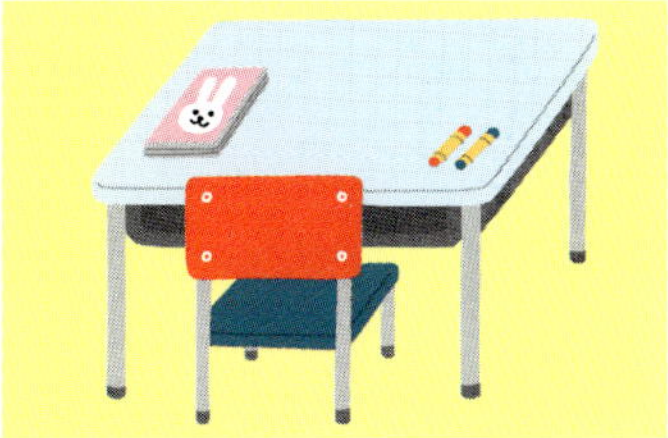

‹ example ›

To parents First, your child will practice pasting with glue. Please cut out the part below for your child. If your child wants to cut it independently, that is okay too. Please assist your child and keep an eye on him or her to avoid any injuries.

■ Paste the cut out part onto the desk.

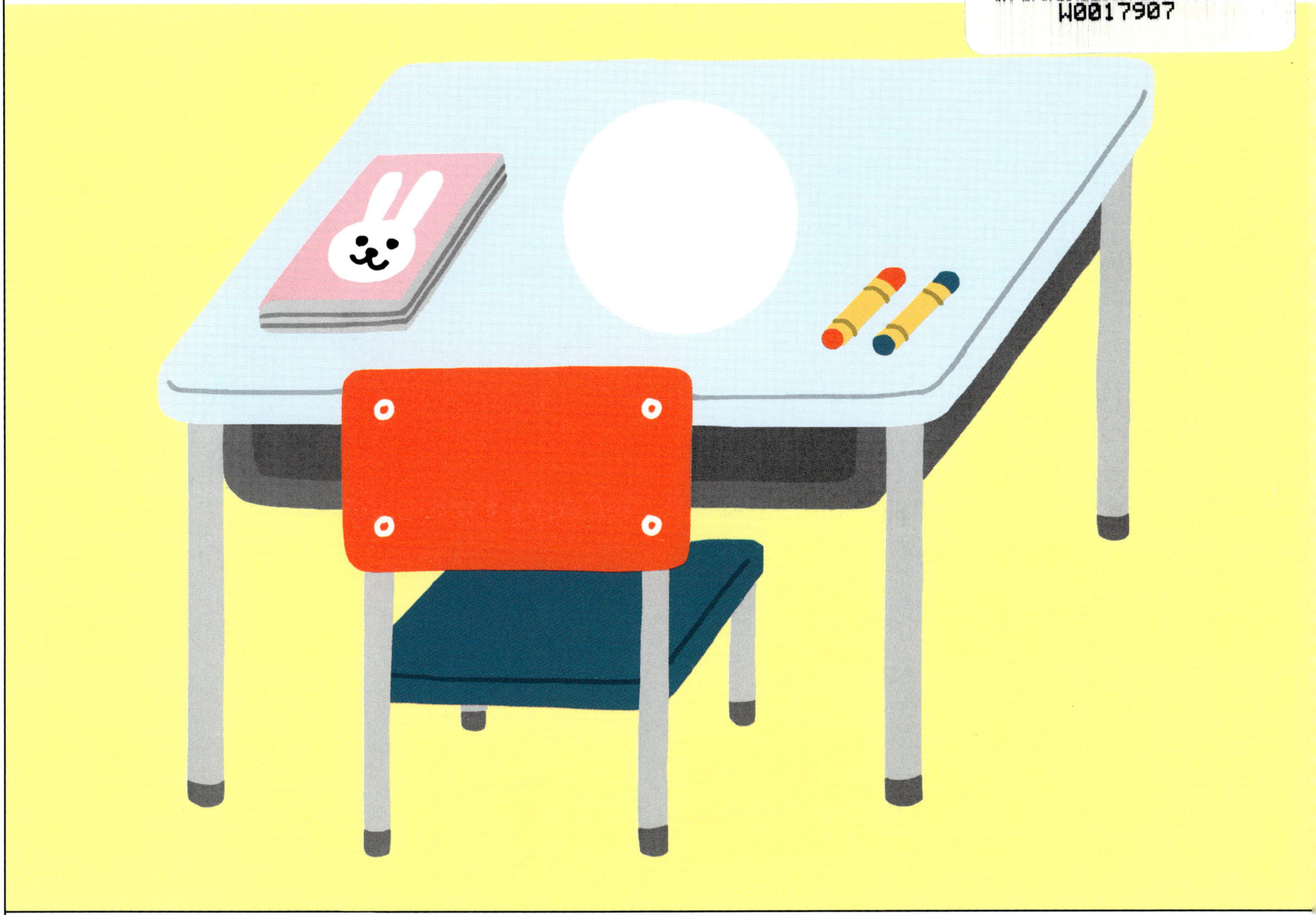

Parents: Please cut along —— for your child.

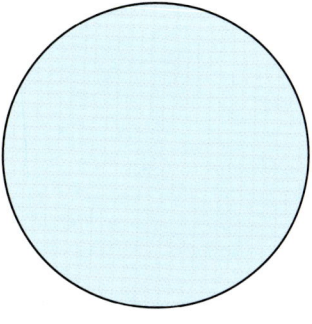

Parents: Please cut this part out for your child.

2 Up and Down the Slide

< example >

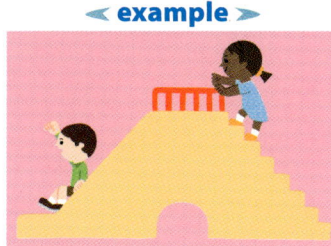

To parents In this exercise, your child will paste the square. Don't be concerned if the cut out piece isn't perfectly placed onto the picture. The most important thing is that your child enjoys pasting with glue.

■ Paste the cut out part onto the slide.

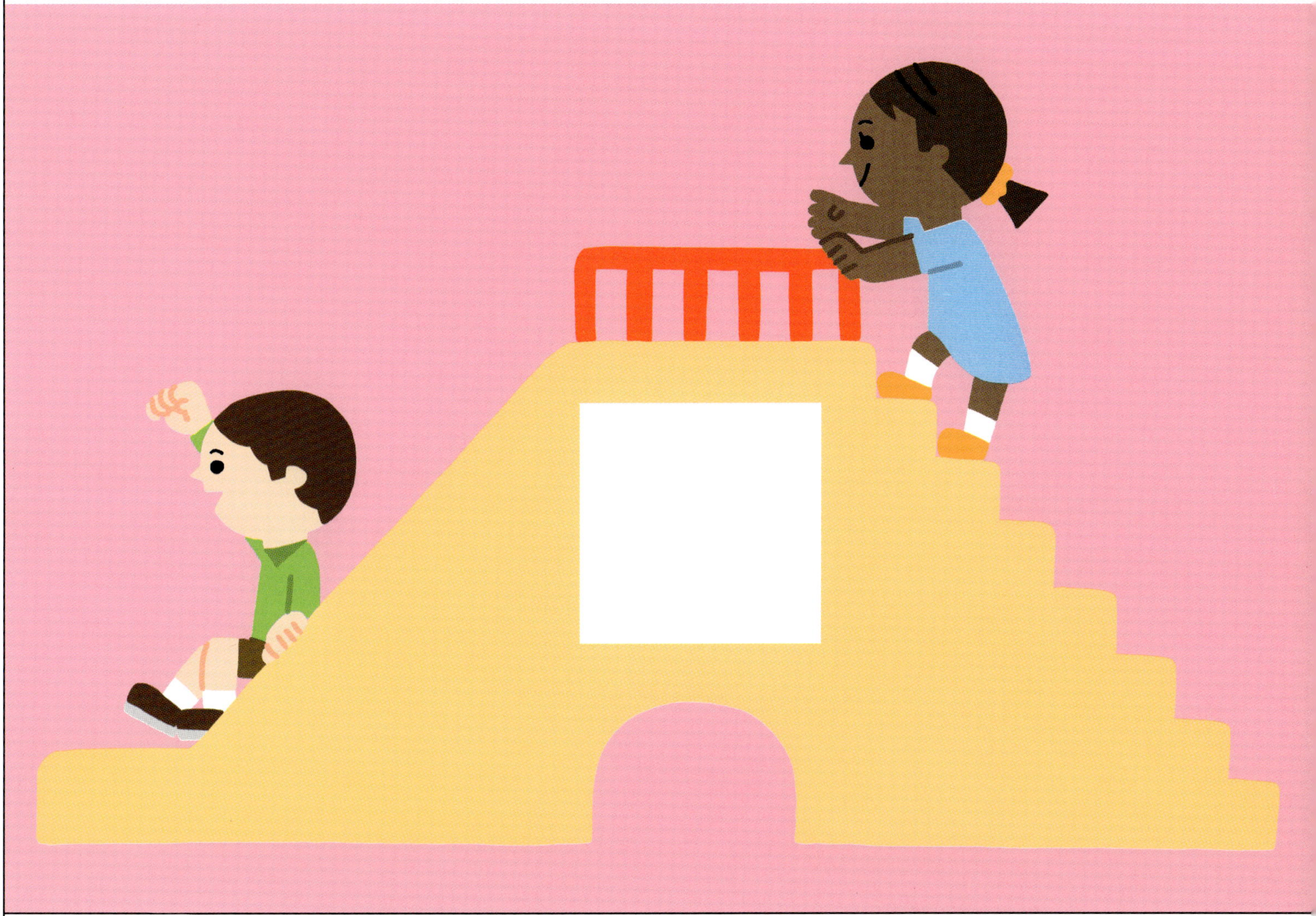

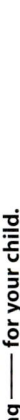

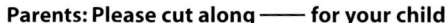

Parents: Please cut along —— for your child.

Parents: Please cut this part out for your child.

Parents: Please cut along —— for your child.

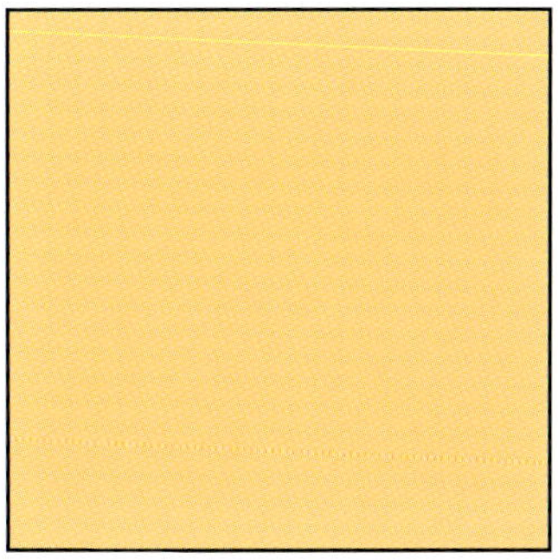

3 Big Tree

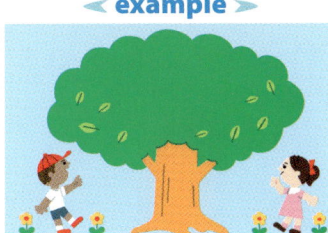

To parents Your child will paste the oval. Encourage your child to pay attention to the orientation of the shape.

example

■ Paste the cut out part onto the tree.

Parents: Please cut along —— for your child.

Parents: Please cut this part out for your child.

Parents: Please cut along —— for your child.

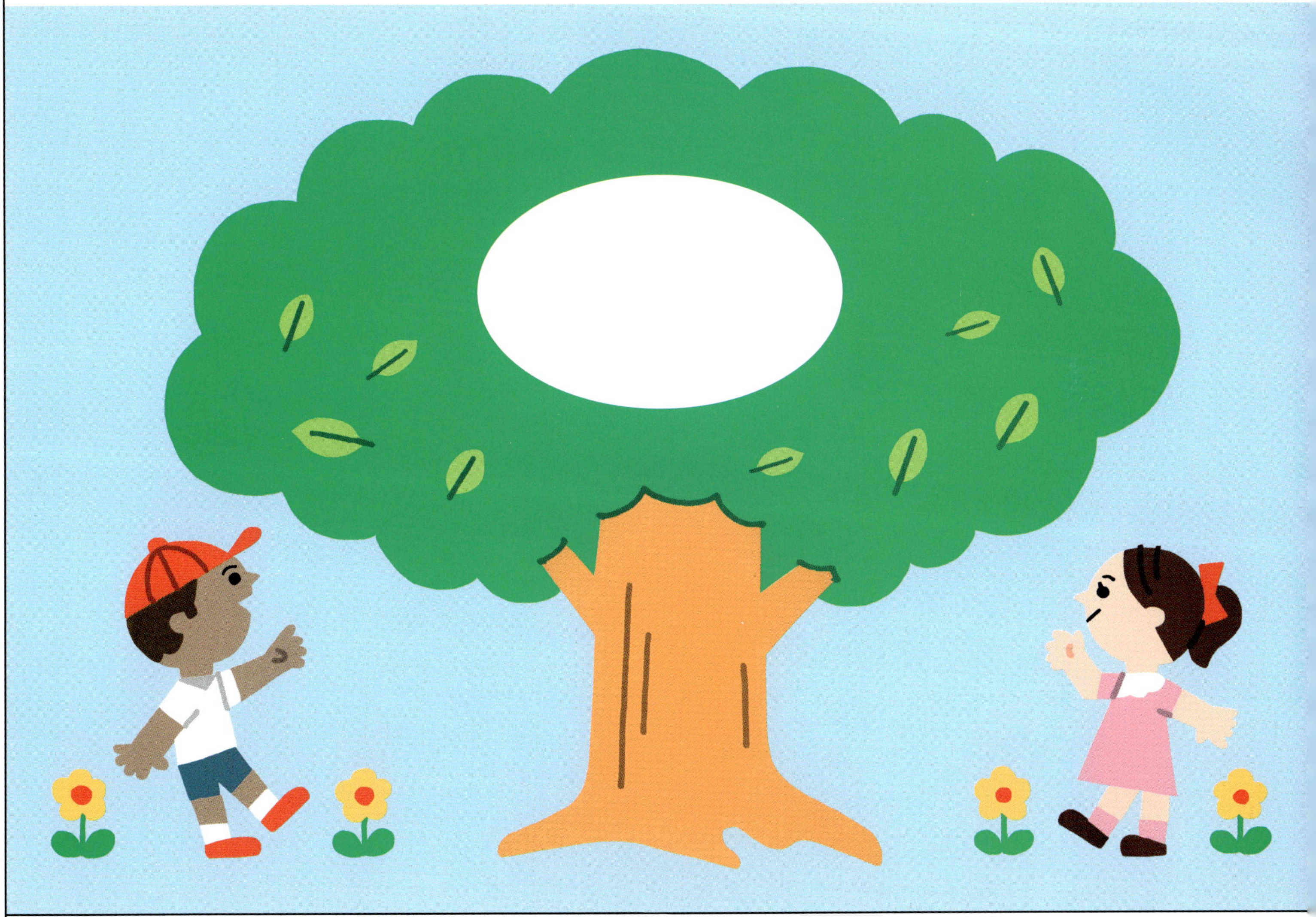

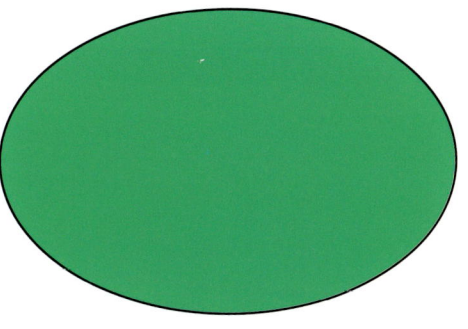

4 Seesaw

< example >

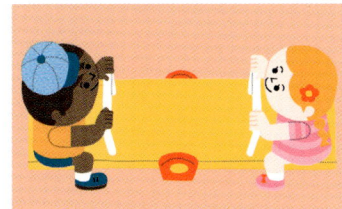

To parents On this page your child will paste the rectangle. Encourage your child to pay attention to the orientation of the shape.

■ Paste the cut out part onto the seesaw.

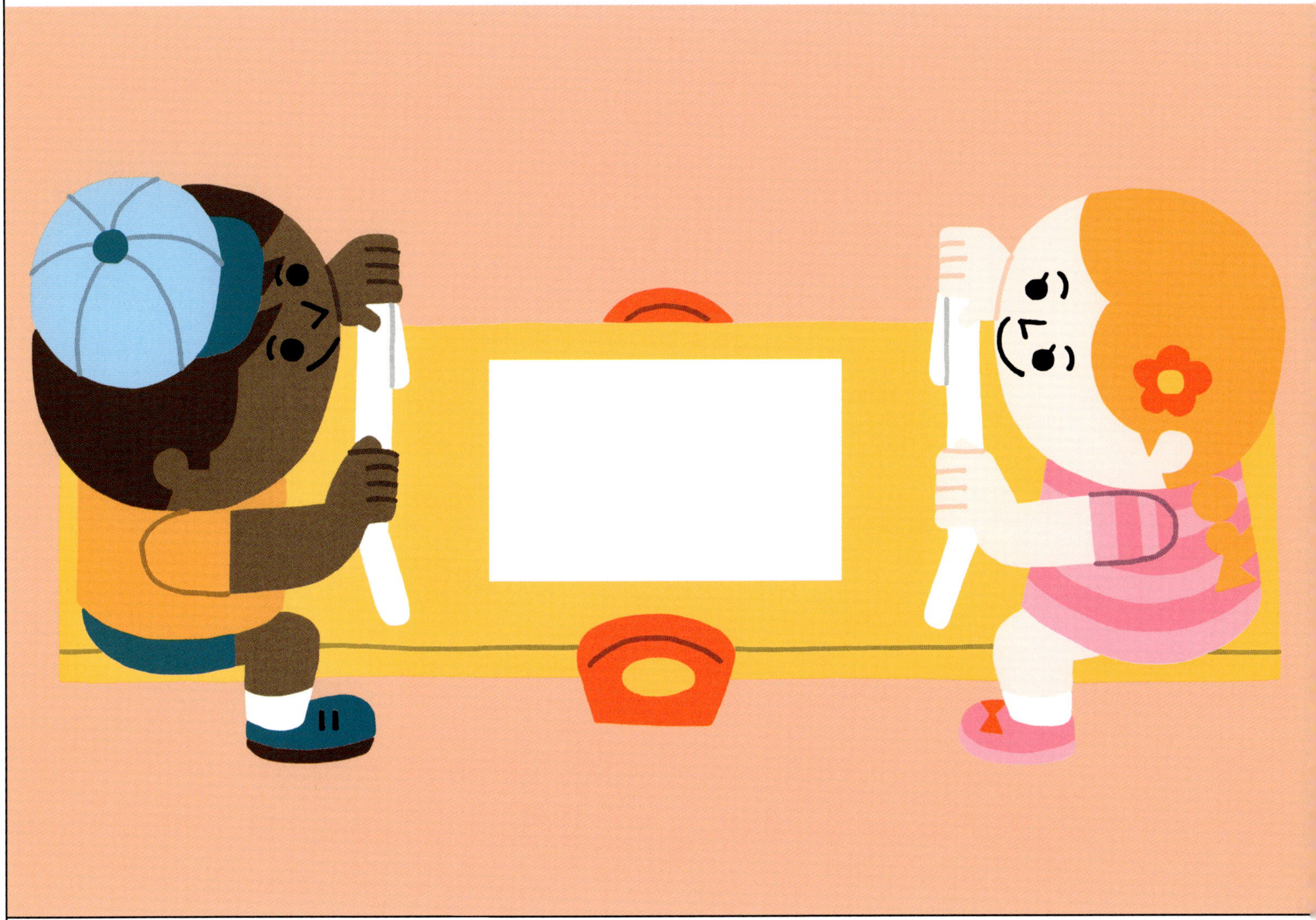

Parents: Please cut along —— for your child.

Parents: Please cut this part out for your child.

Parents: Please cut along —— for your child.

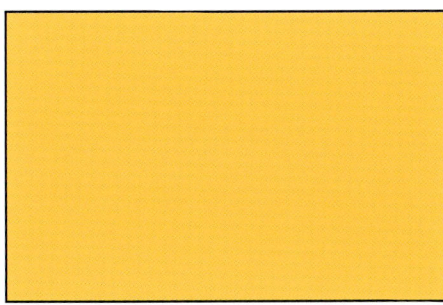

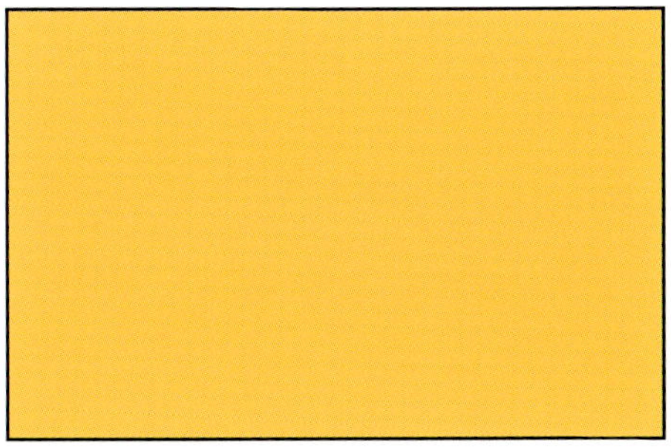

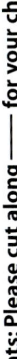

5 Turtles In a Pond

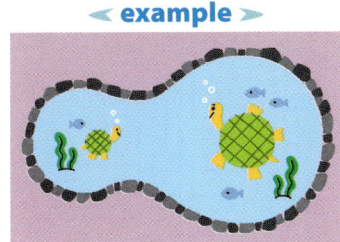

To parents Your child will paste the triangle. Don't be concerned if the cut out piece isn't perfectly placed onto the picture—this page requires intricate work. When he or she is finished, praise your child's work.

< example >

■ Paste the cut out part onto the pond.

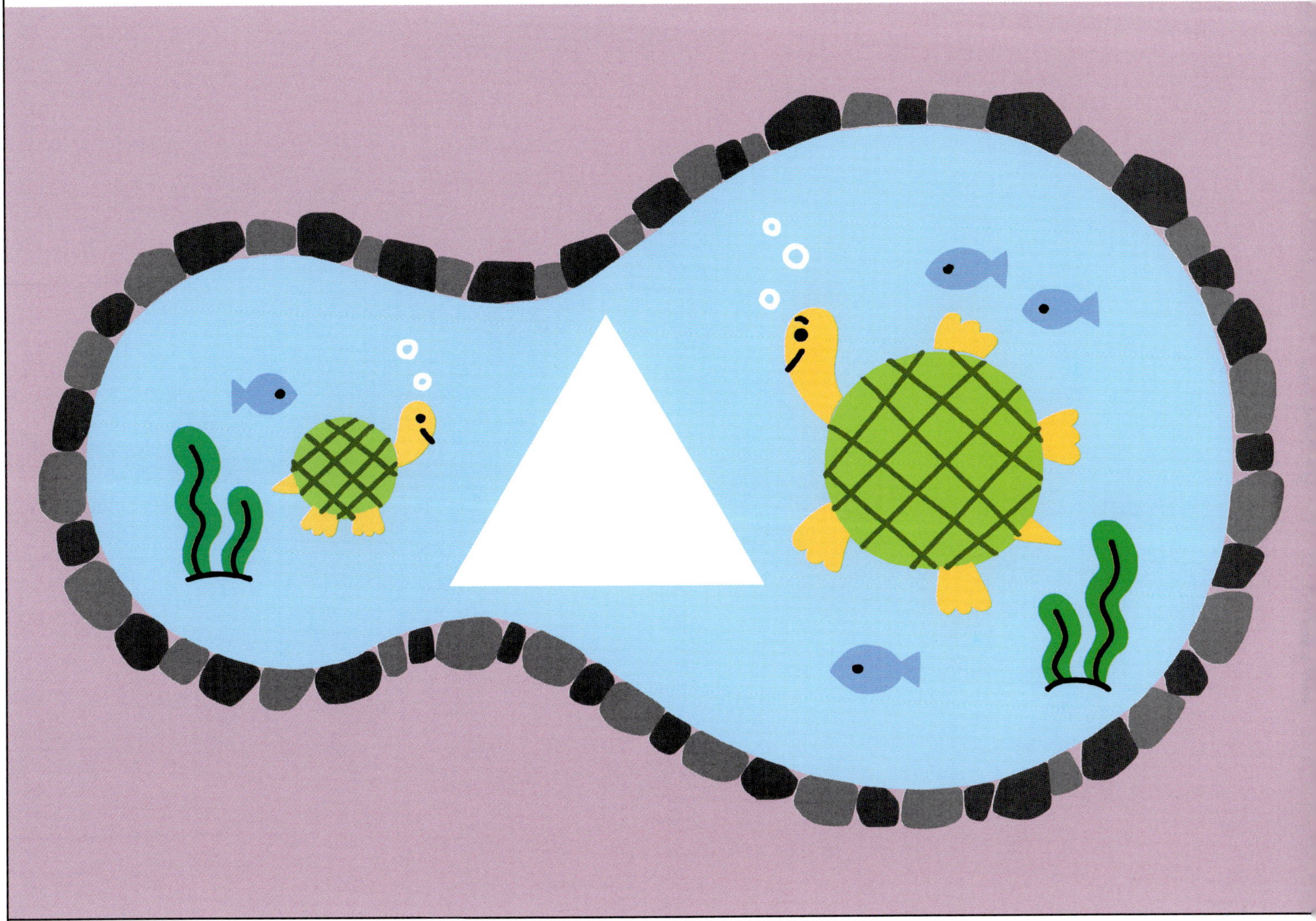

Parents: Please cut along —— for your child.

Parents: Please cut this part out for your child.

Parents: Please cut along —— for your child.

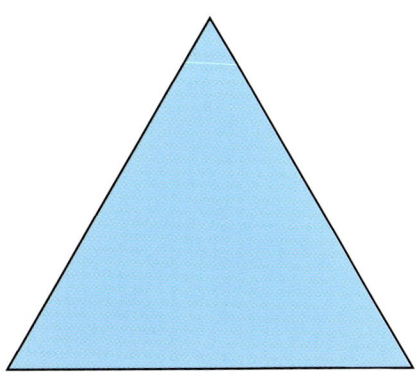

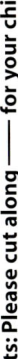

6 Kindergarten

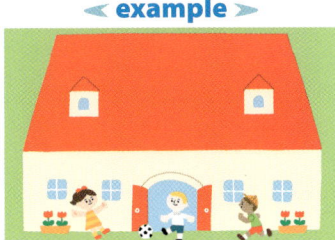

< example >

To parents Your child should be careful to correctly align the piece. If he or she doesn't know the proper orientation, please offer to help.

■ Paste the cut out part onto the roof.

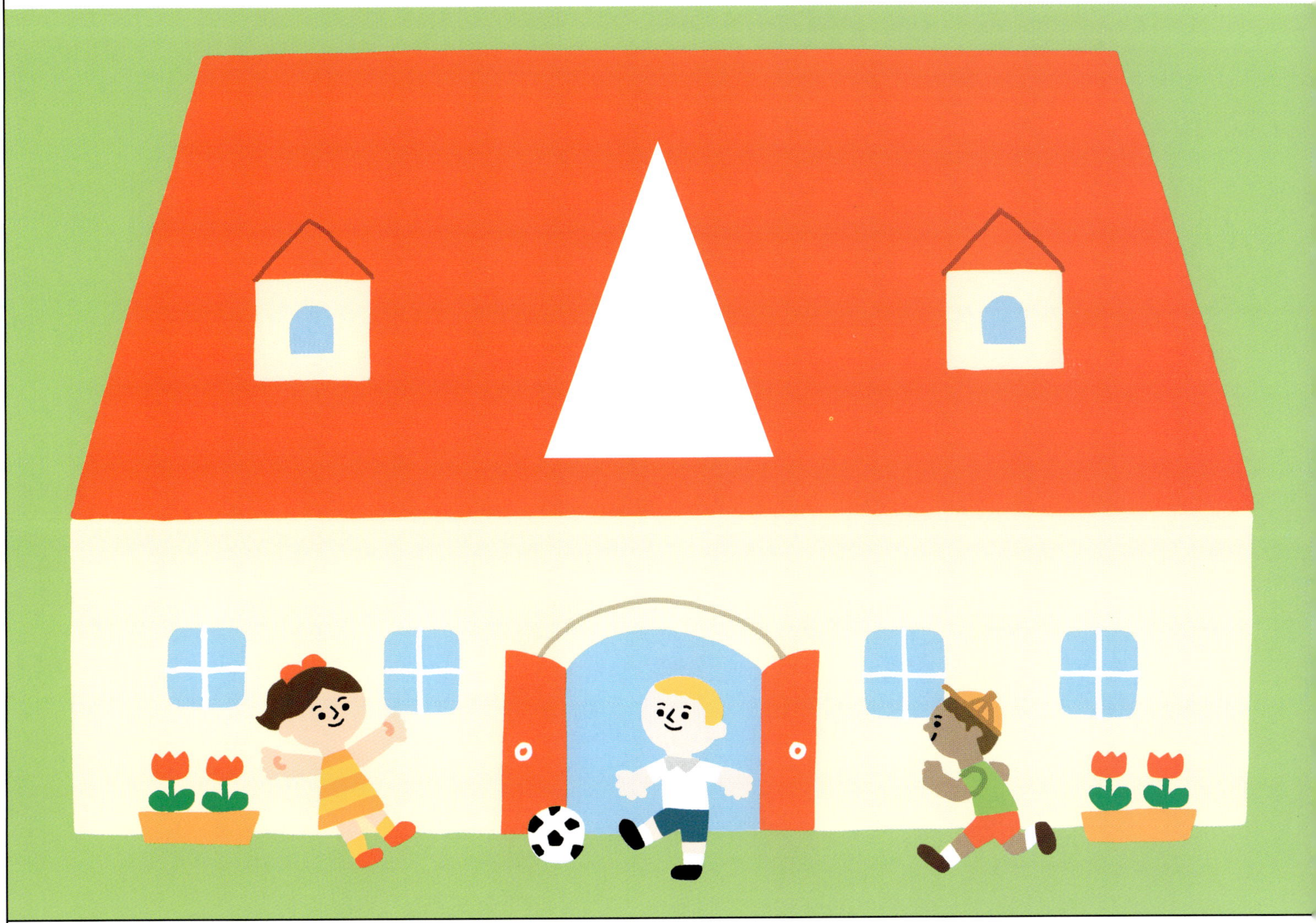

Parents: Please cut along —— for your child.

Parents: Please cut this part out for your child.

Parents: Please cut along —— for your child.

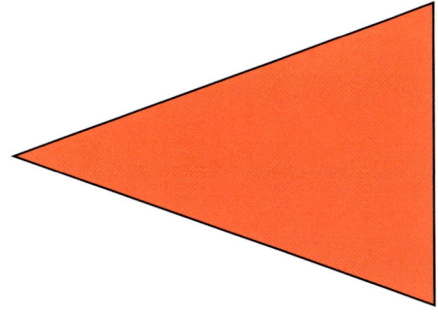

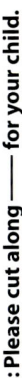

7 My Bag

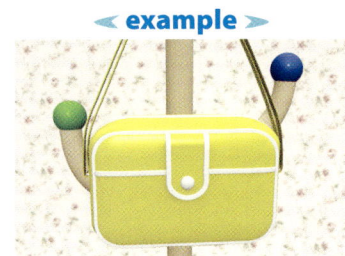

< example >

To parents From this page on, your child will practice pasting to complete the design in the picture. If the piece isn't placed onto the picture neatly, don't be concerned.

■ Paste the cut out part onto the bag.

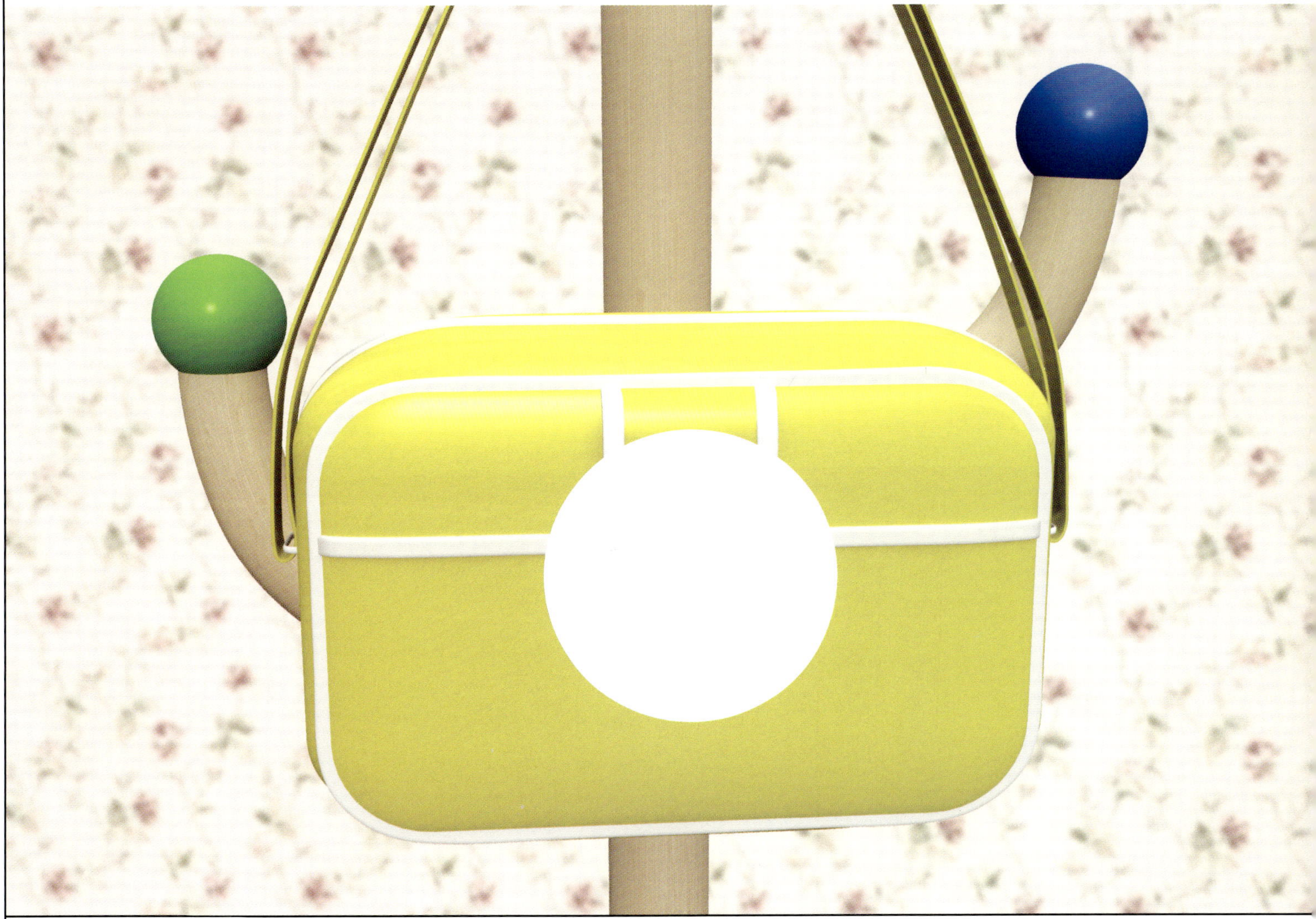

Parents: Please cut along —— for your child.

Parents: Please cut this part out for your child.

Parents: Please cut along —— for your child.

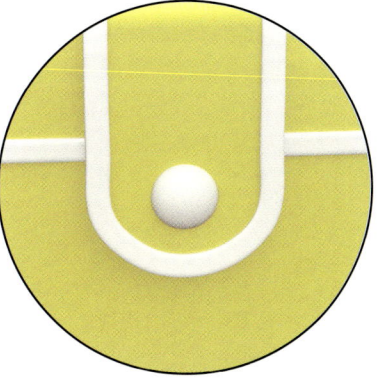

8 My Hat

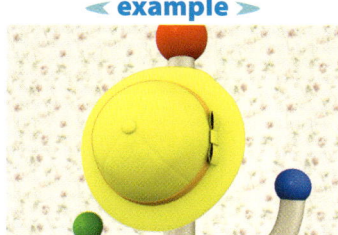

To parents The most important thing is that your child enjoys pasting. When he or she is finished, talk about the hats your child likes to wear.

< example >

■ Paste the cut out part onto the hat.

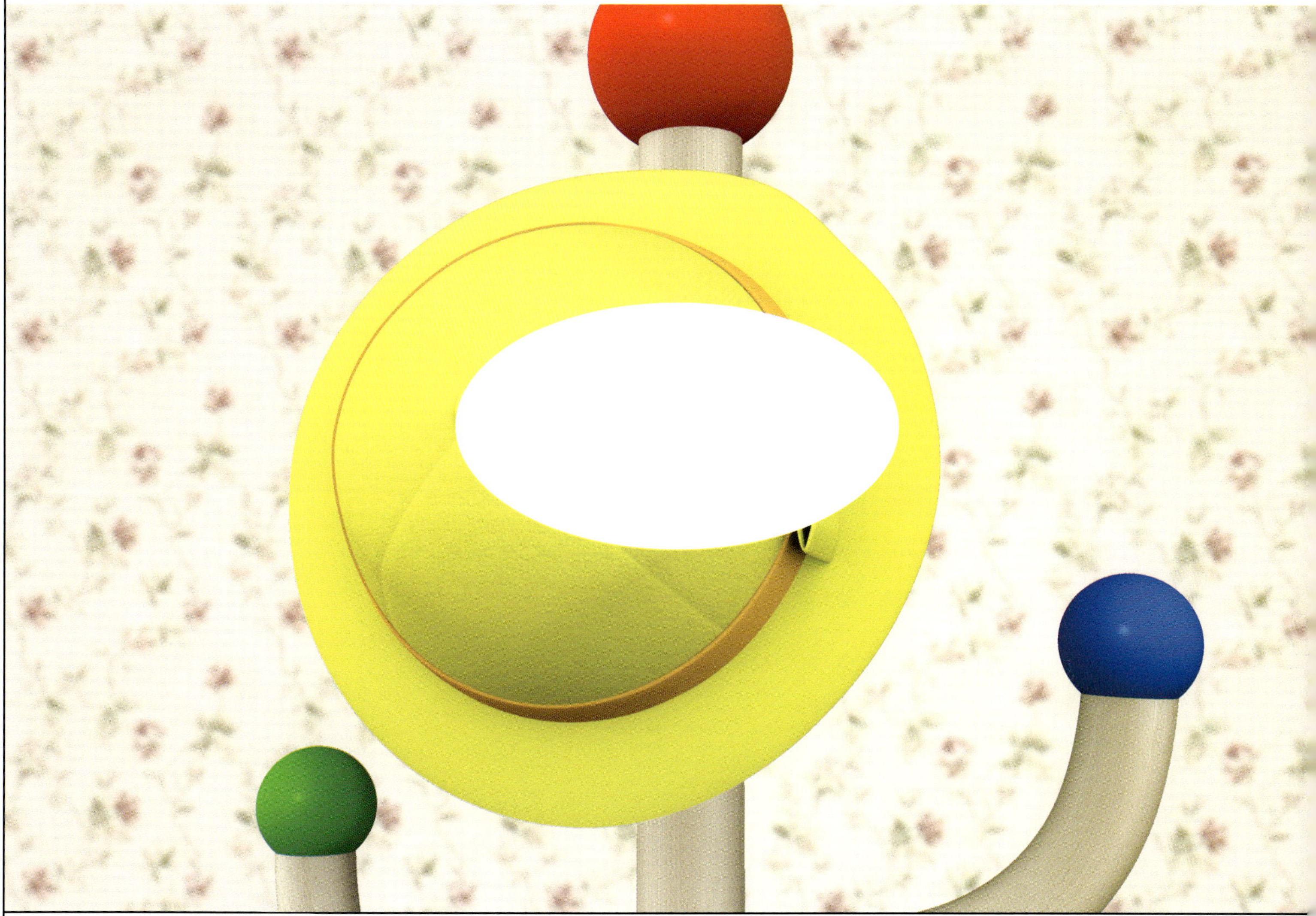

Parents: Please cut along —— for your child.

Parents: Please cut this part out for your child.

Parents: Please cut along —— for your child.

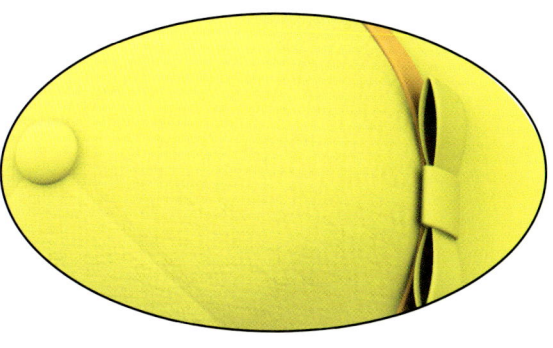

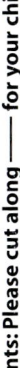

9 Bear's Mug

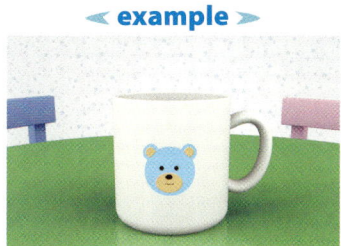

example

To parents On this page your child must paste the piece with the bear's face in the correct orientation. It helps to discuss the proper placement with your child before he or she pastes the part.

Paste the cut out part onto the mug.

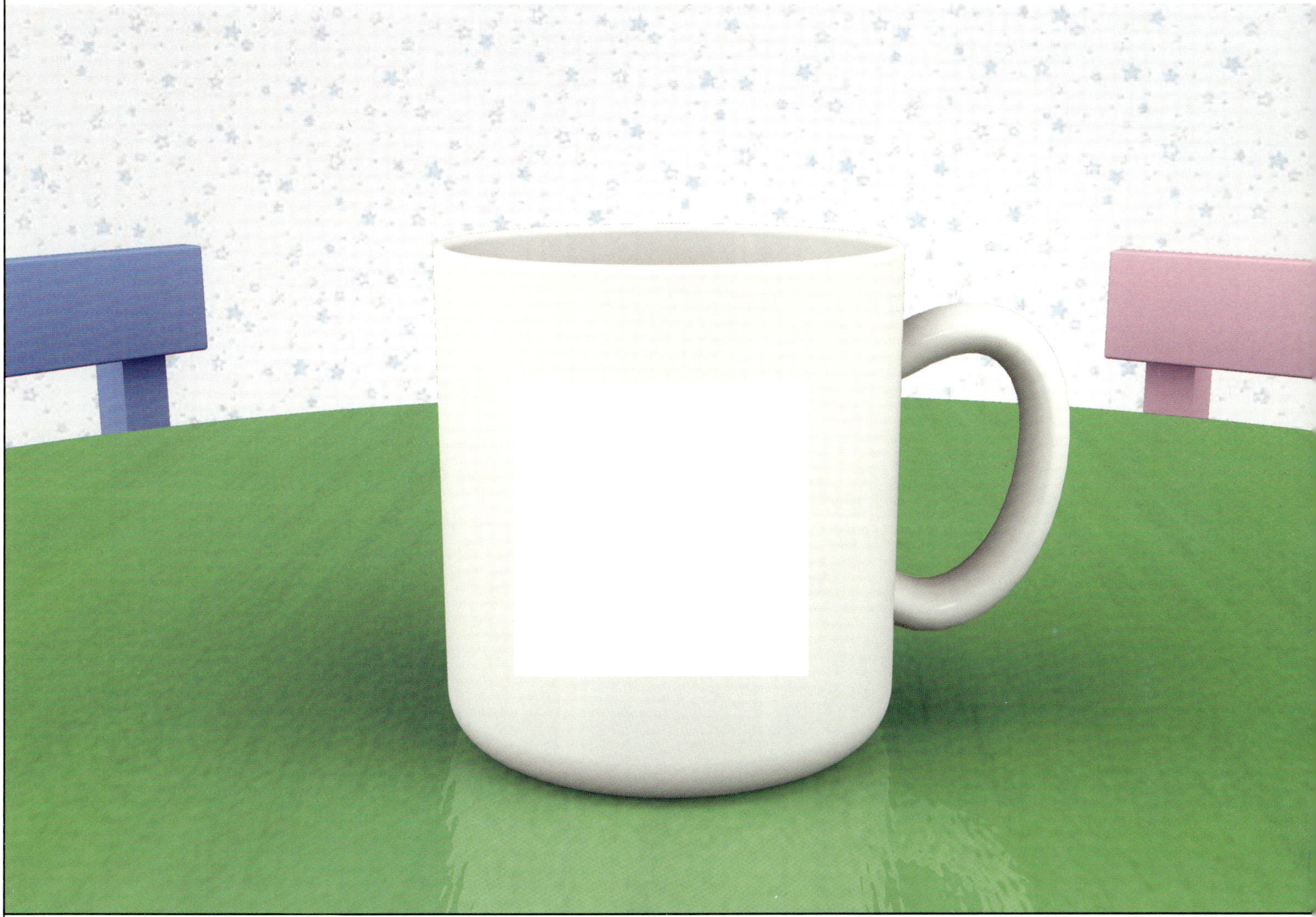

Parents: Please cut along —— for your child.

Parents: Please cut this part out for your child.

Parents: Please cut along —— for your child.

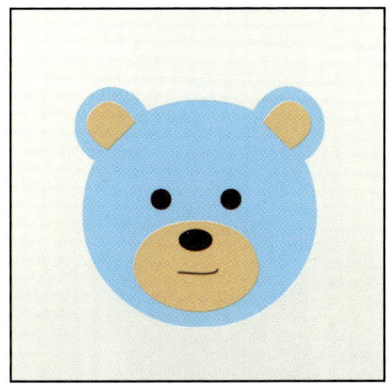

10 Frog's Umbrella

< example >

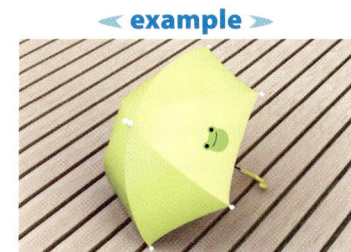

To parents This exercise encourages your child to practice pasting parts with the correct orientation. Please help your child place the frog's face in the appropriate position.

■ Paste the cut out part onto the umbrella.

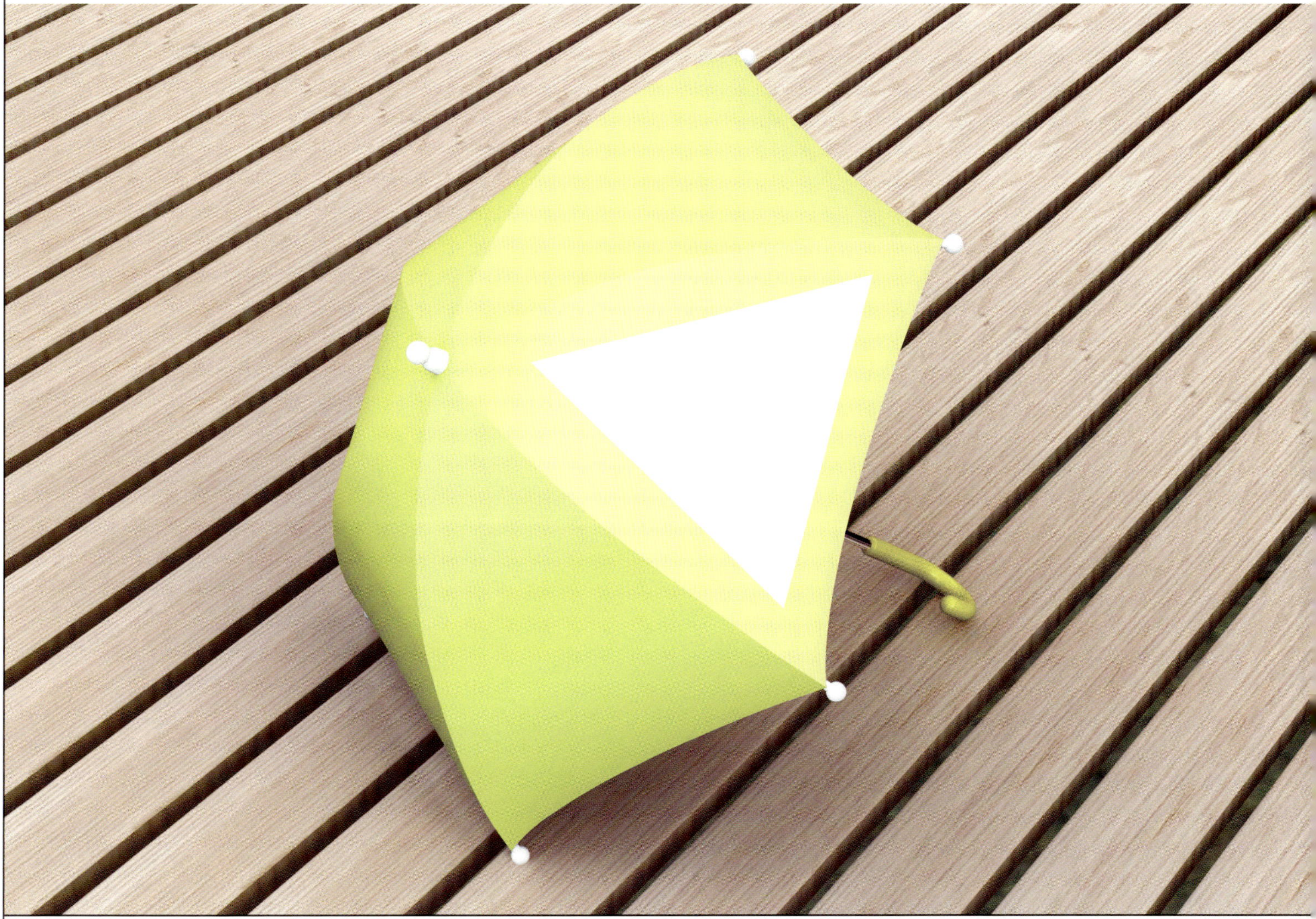

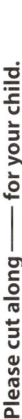

Parents: Please cut along —— for your child.

Parents: Please cut this part out for your child.

Parents: Please cut along —— for your child.

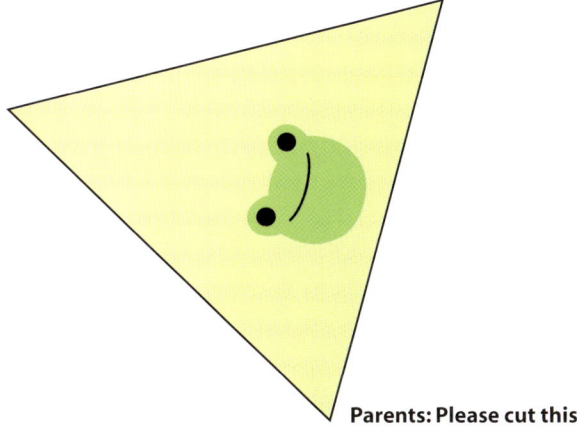

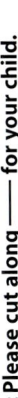

11 Rabbit's Towel

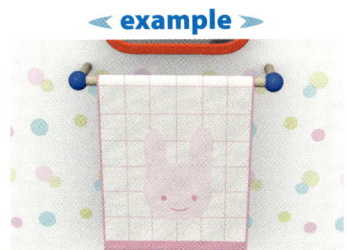

To parents This towel has an intricate pattern. If the pattern on the towel doesn't perfectly match the pasted part, don't be concerned. When your child is finished, offer a lot of praise.

■ Paste the cut out part onto the towel.

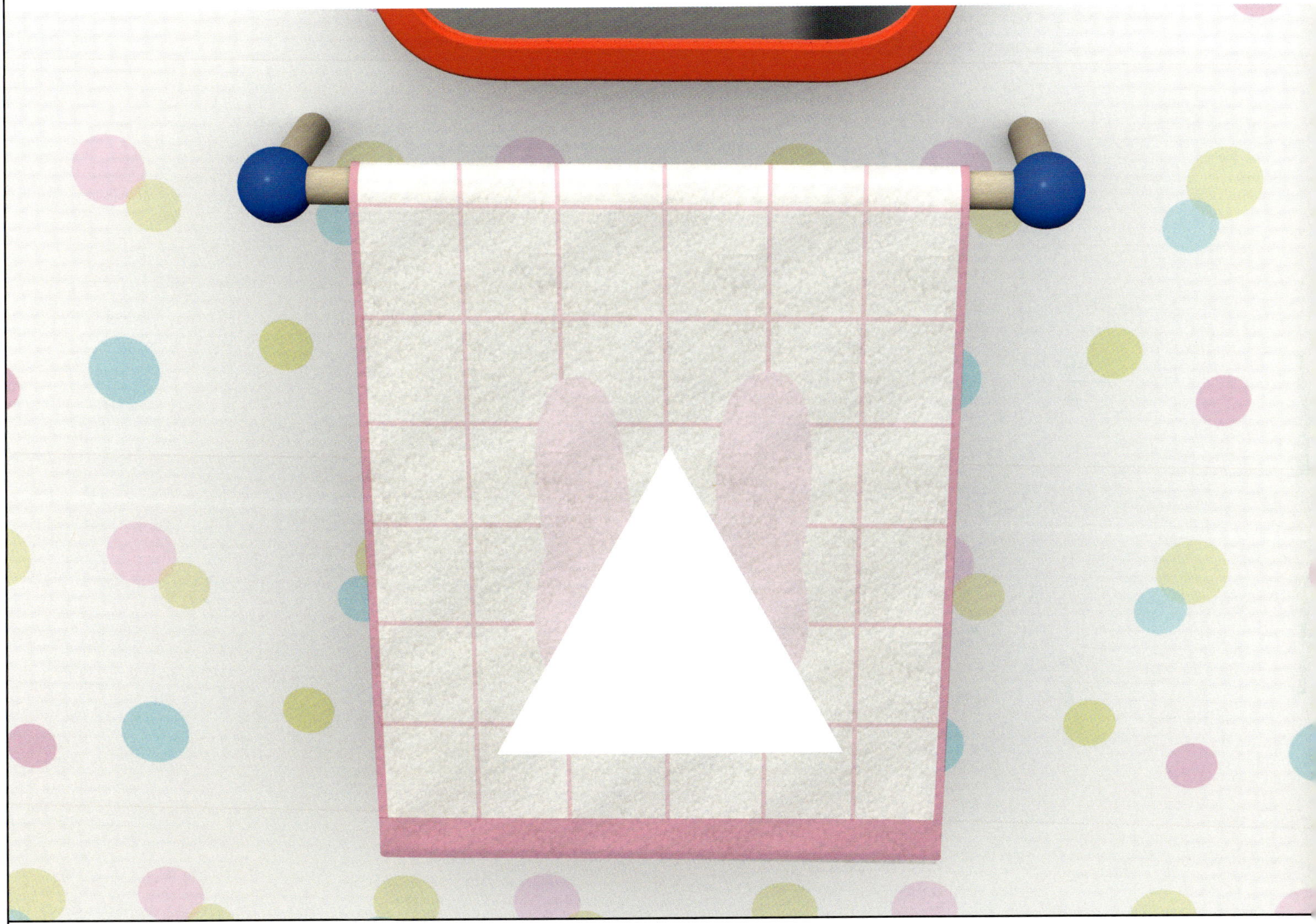

Parents: Please cut along —— for your child.

Parents: Please cut this part out for your child.

Parents: Please cut along —— for your child.

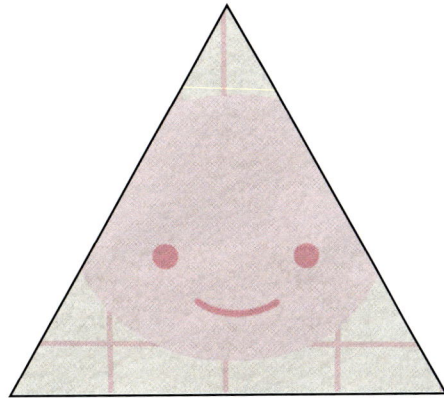

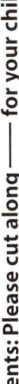

12 Frog's Rain Boots

< example >

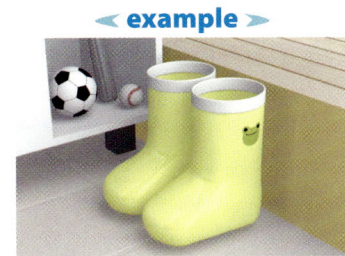

To parents Your child will paste the piece to complete the rain boots. It is difficult to perfectly match the illustration. If it isn't correctly placed onto the picture, don't be concerned.

■ Paste the cut out part onto the rain boots.

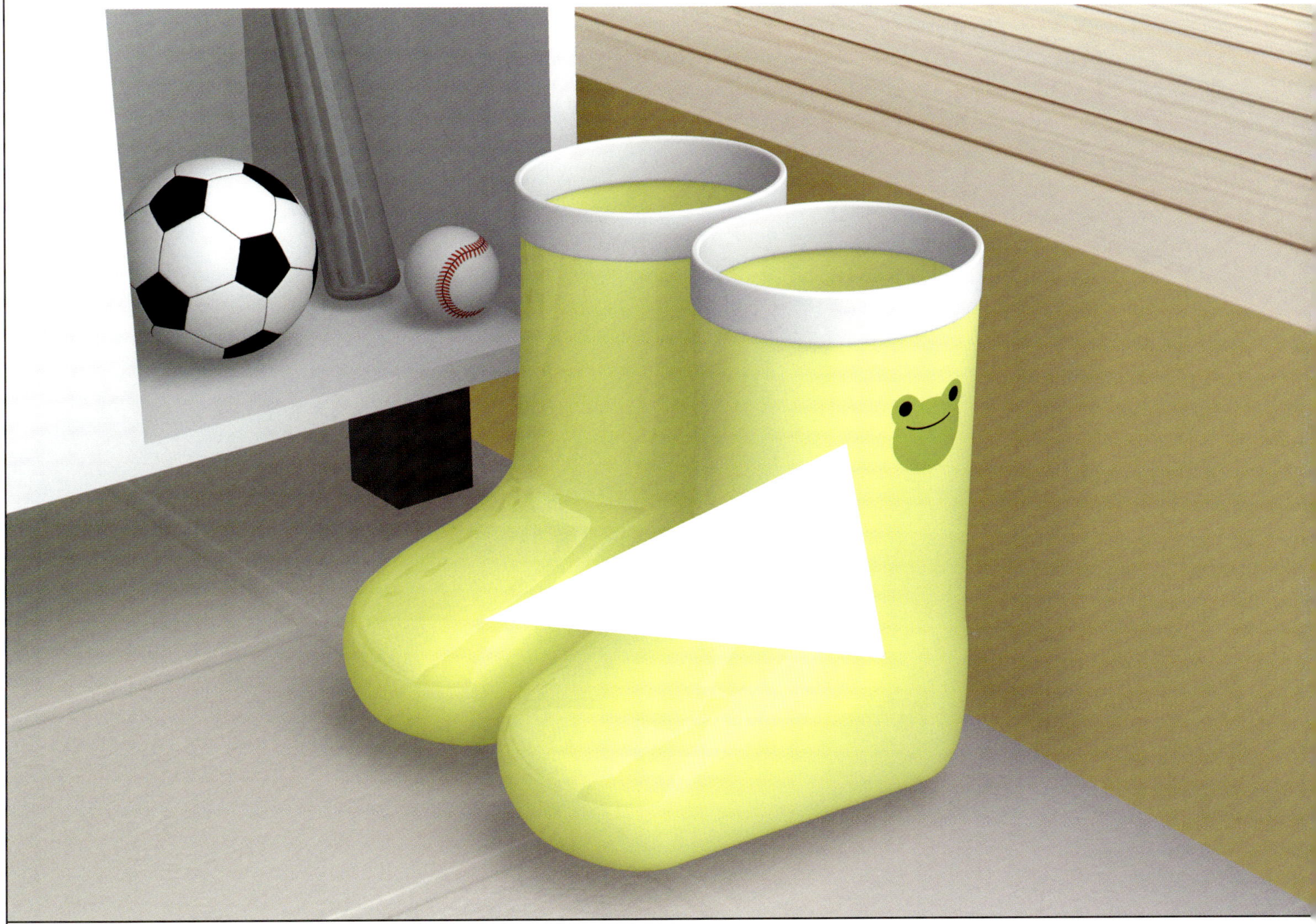

Parents: Please cut along —— for your child.

Parents: Please cut this part out for your child.

Parents: Please cut along —— for your child.

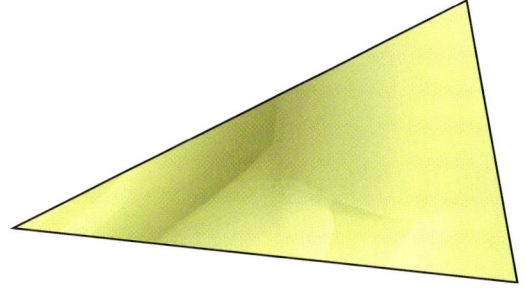

 **Playing Ball**

< example >

To parents From this page on, your child will practice pasting pieces onto the page wherever he or she likes. An example is offered but please allow your child to paste freely.

■ Paste the ball as you like.

Parents: Please cut along —— for your child.

Parents: Please cut along —— for your child.

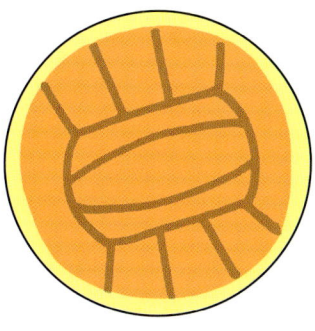

Parents: Please cut this part out for your child.

14 Drawing a Picture

To parents In this exercise your child will paste the crayons onto the desk. If your child doesn't know where to place the piece, offer to help.

example

■ Paste the crayons on the desk as you like.

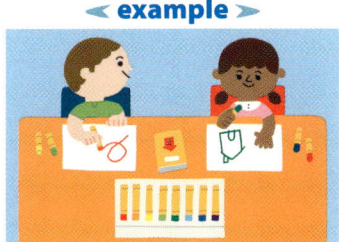

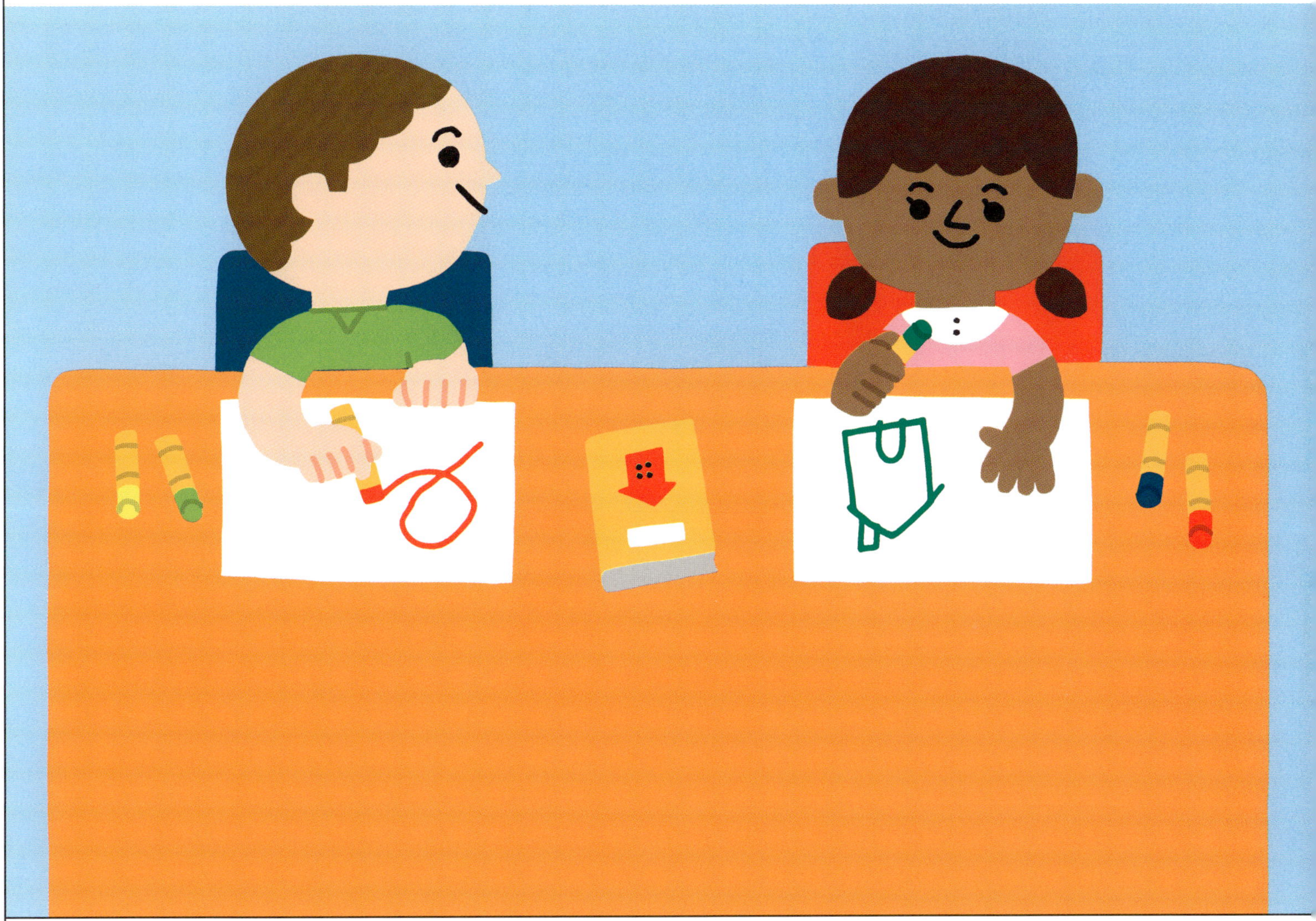

Parents: Please cut along —— for your child.

Parents: Please cut this part out for your child.

Parents: Please cut along —— for your child.

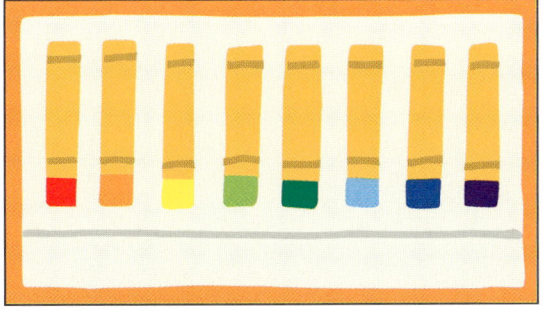

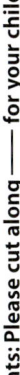

15 Put the Shoes Away

To parents Your child will paste the shoes onto the cubby. There are more empty cubbyholes than the amount of pieces. Encourage your child to paste the shoes on whichever empty cubbyholes that he or she likes.

< example >

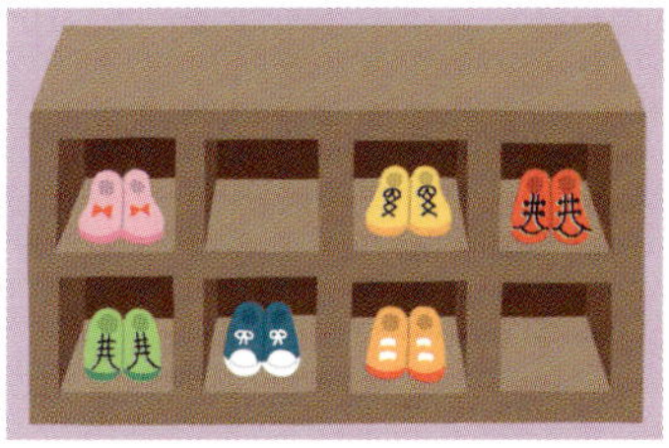

■ Paste the shoes onto the cubby as you like.

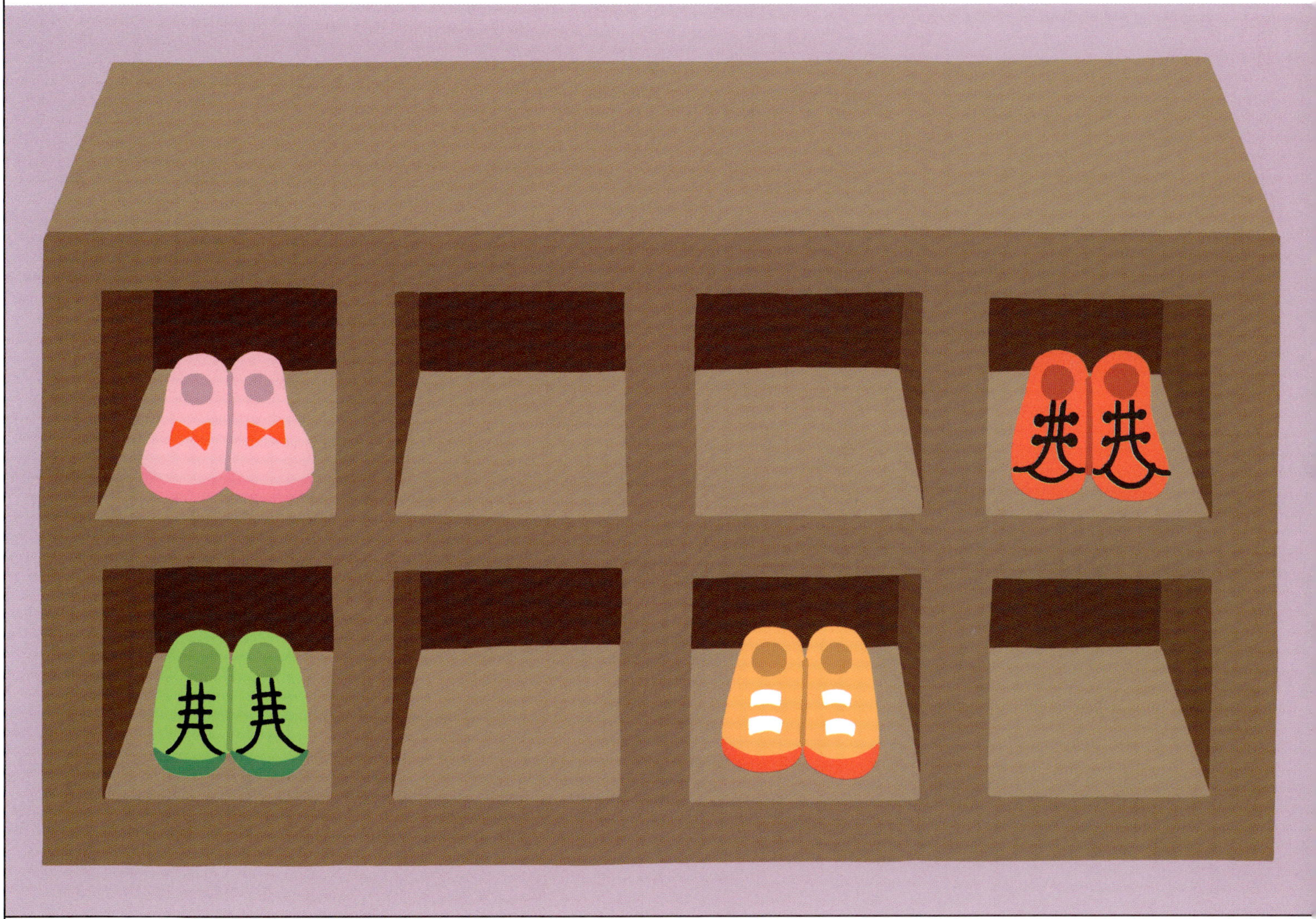

Parents: Please cut along —— for your child.

Parents: Please cut these parts out for your child.

Parents: Please cut along —— for your child.

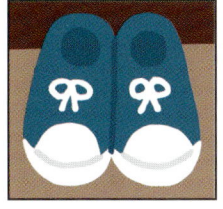

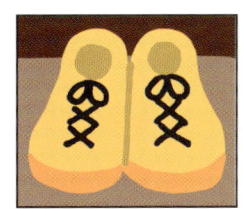

Birthday Party

< example >

To parents If your child doesn't know where to place the piece, ask, "Who is not wearing a hat?"
Please remember to praise your child for his or her hard work.

■ Paste the hats as you like.

Parents: Please cut along ——— for your child.

Parents: Please cut along ——— for your child.

Parents: Please cut these parts out for your child.

17 Let's Get Dressed

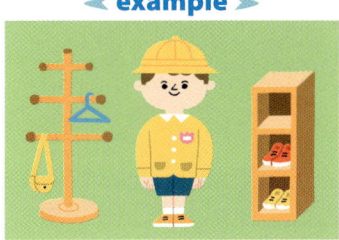

< example >

To parents Your child will paste the clothes, hat and shoes. When he or she is finished, offer a lot of praise and then say, "Can you put on your clothes by yourself?"

■ Paste the clothes onto the boy.

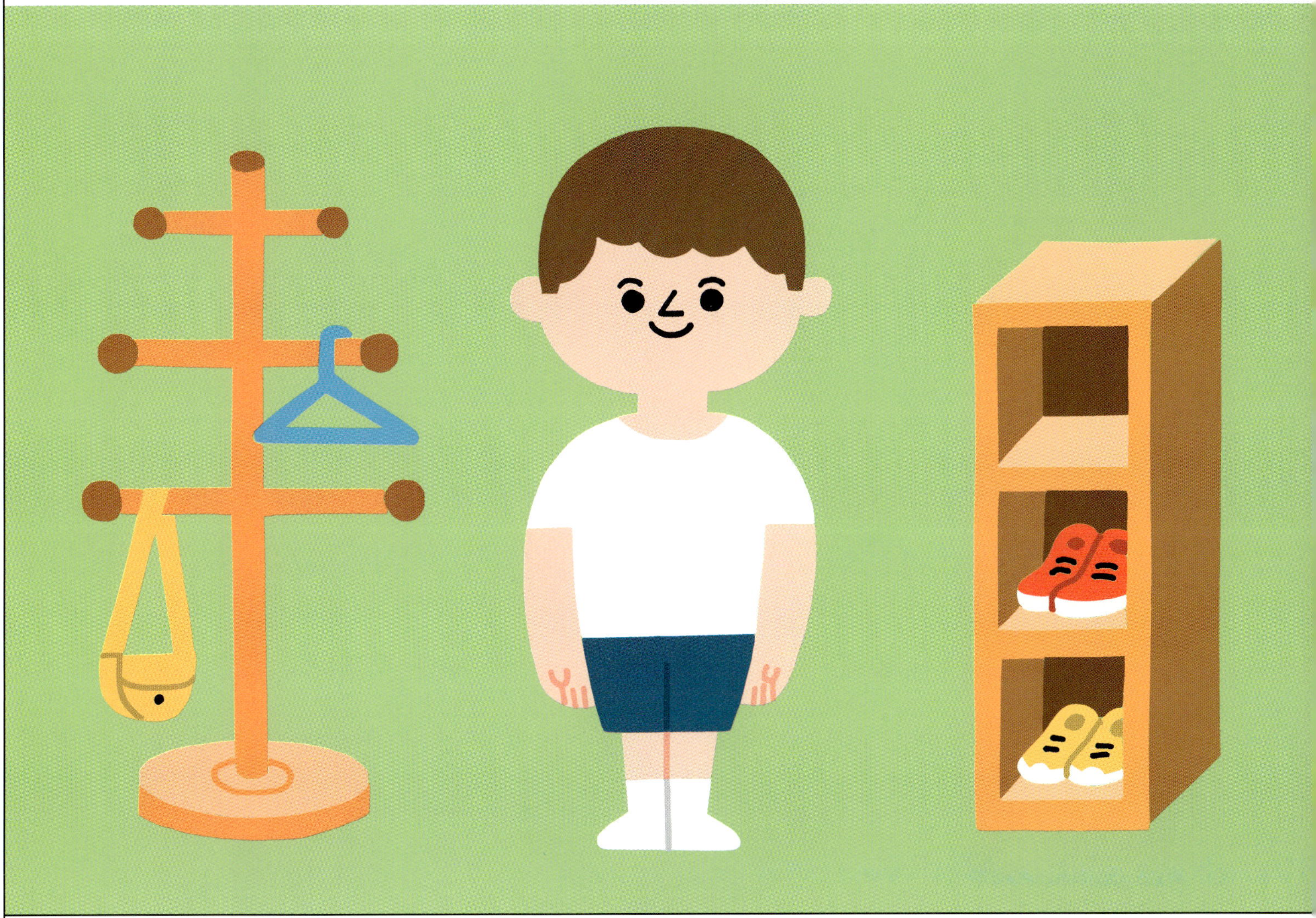

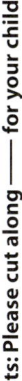

Parents: Please cut along —— for your child.

Parents: Please cut these parts out for your child.

Parents: Please cut along —— for your child.

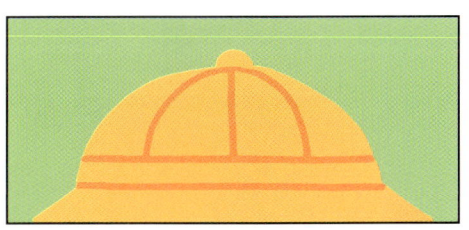

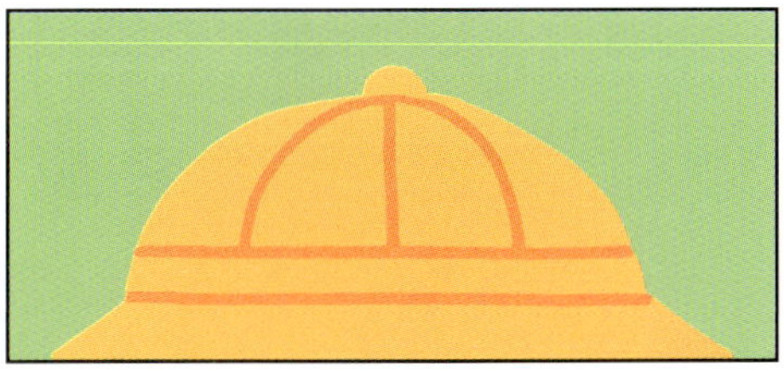

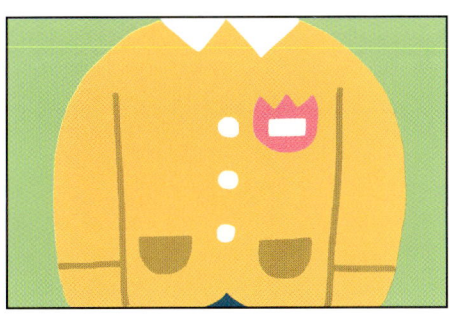

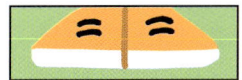

 **Art Supplies**

< **example** >

To parents Your child will paste the art supplies as though they are putting the items away in the box.
When he or she is finished, offer a lot of praise, such as, "You put the supplies away very well."

■ Paste the craft supplies into the box as you like.

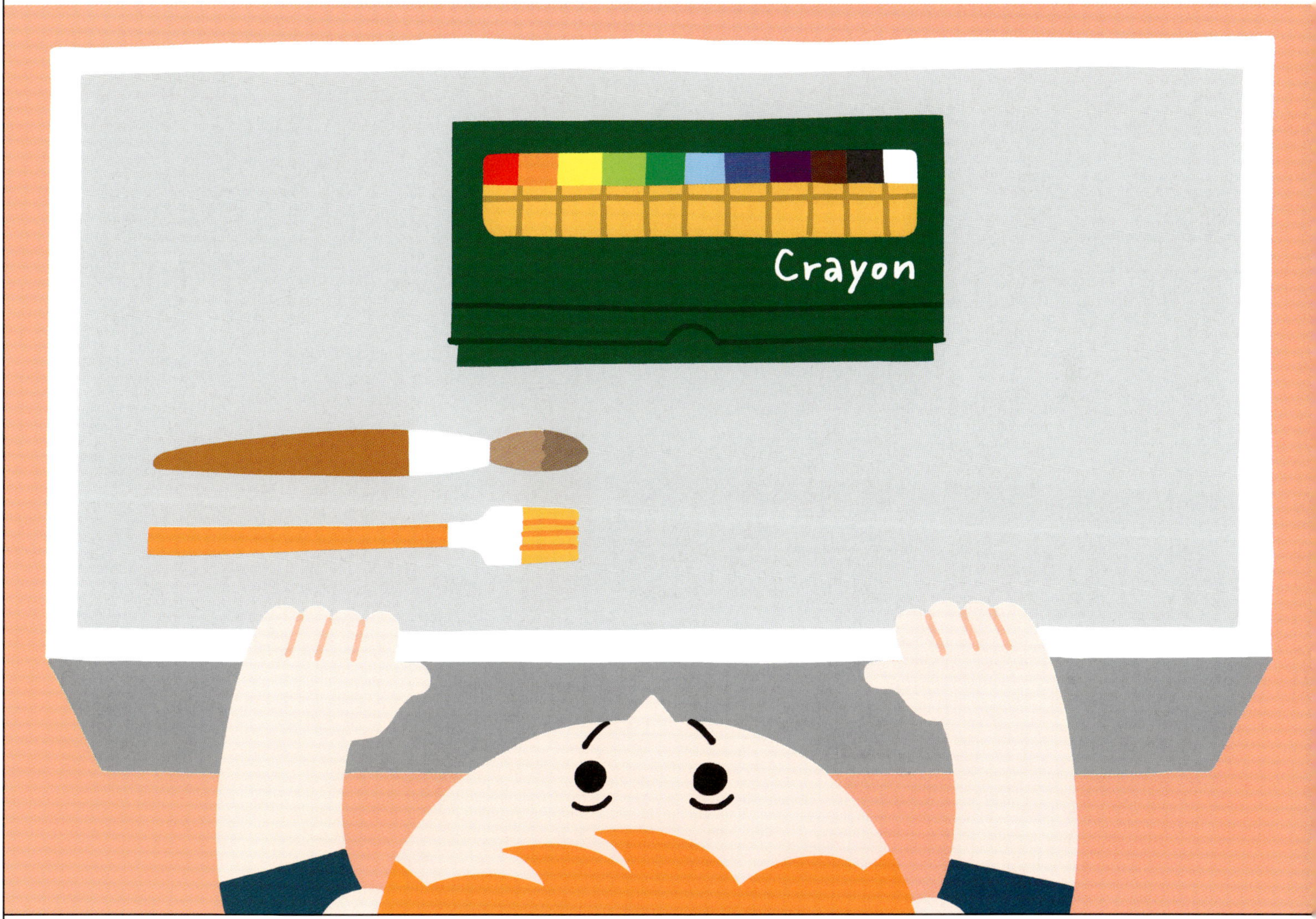

Parents: Please cut along —— for your child.

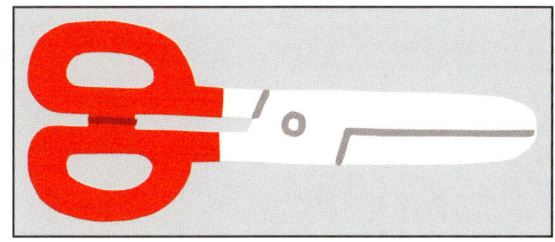

Parents: Please cut these parts out for your child.

Put the Toys Away

< **example** >

■ Paste the cut out parts onto the cubby as you like.

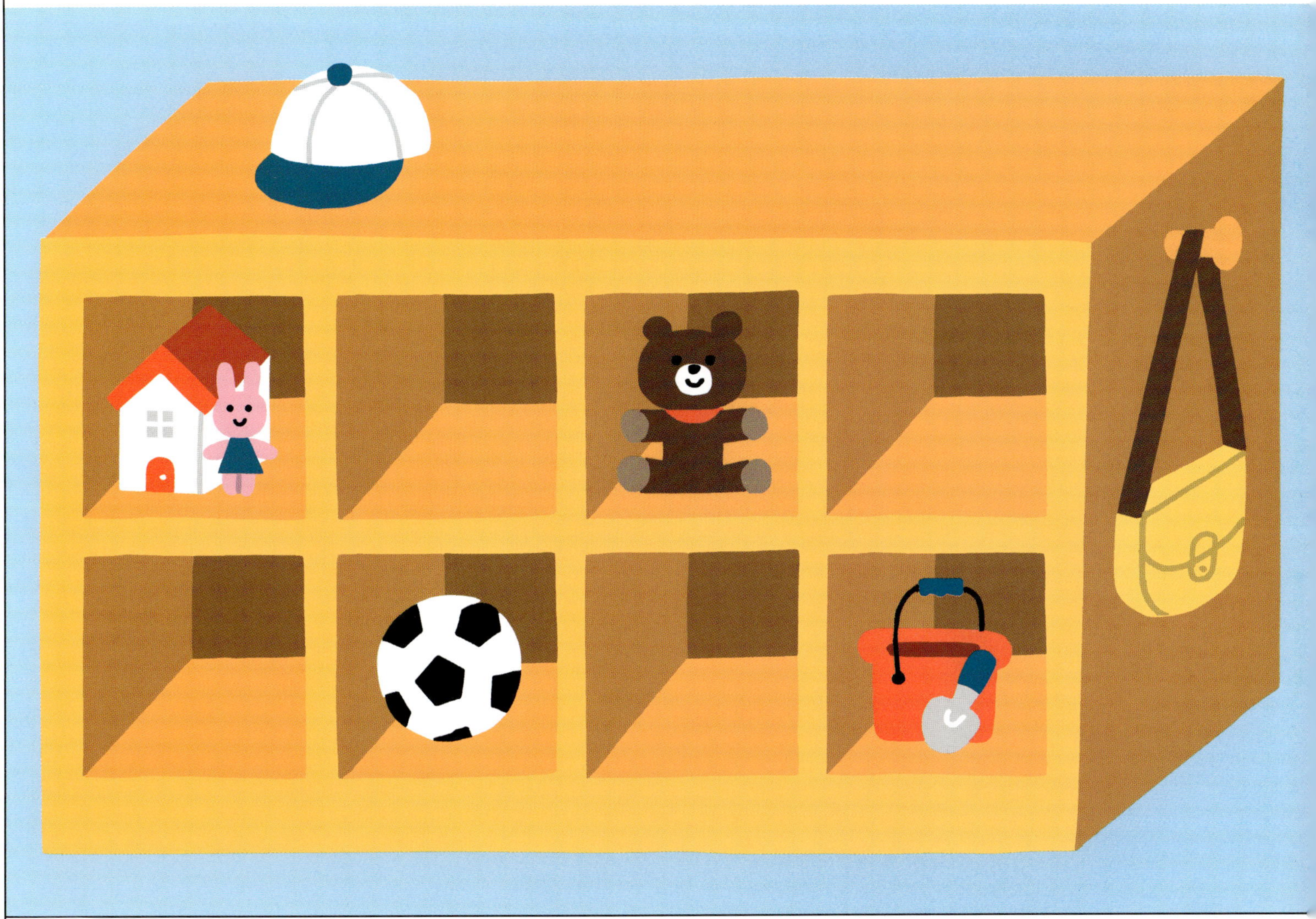

Parents: Please cut along —— for your child.

Parents: Please cut these parts out for your child.

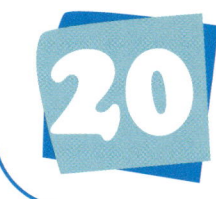

20 What Time Is It Now?

< example >

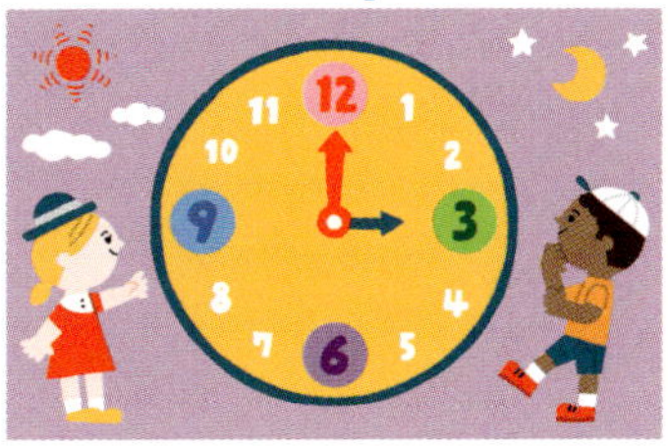

To parents Your child will paste the numbers onto the clock. If he or she doesn't know the correct place to paste each number, offer to help. When the clock is finished, read the numbers in order to your child and talk about the time.

■ Paste the numbers onto the clock.

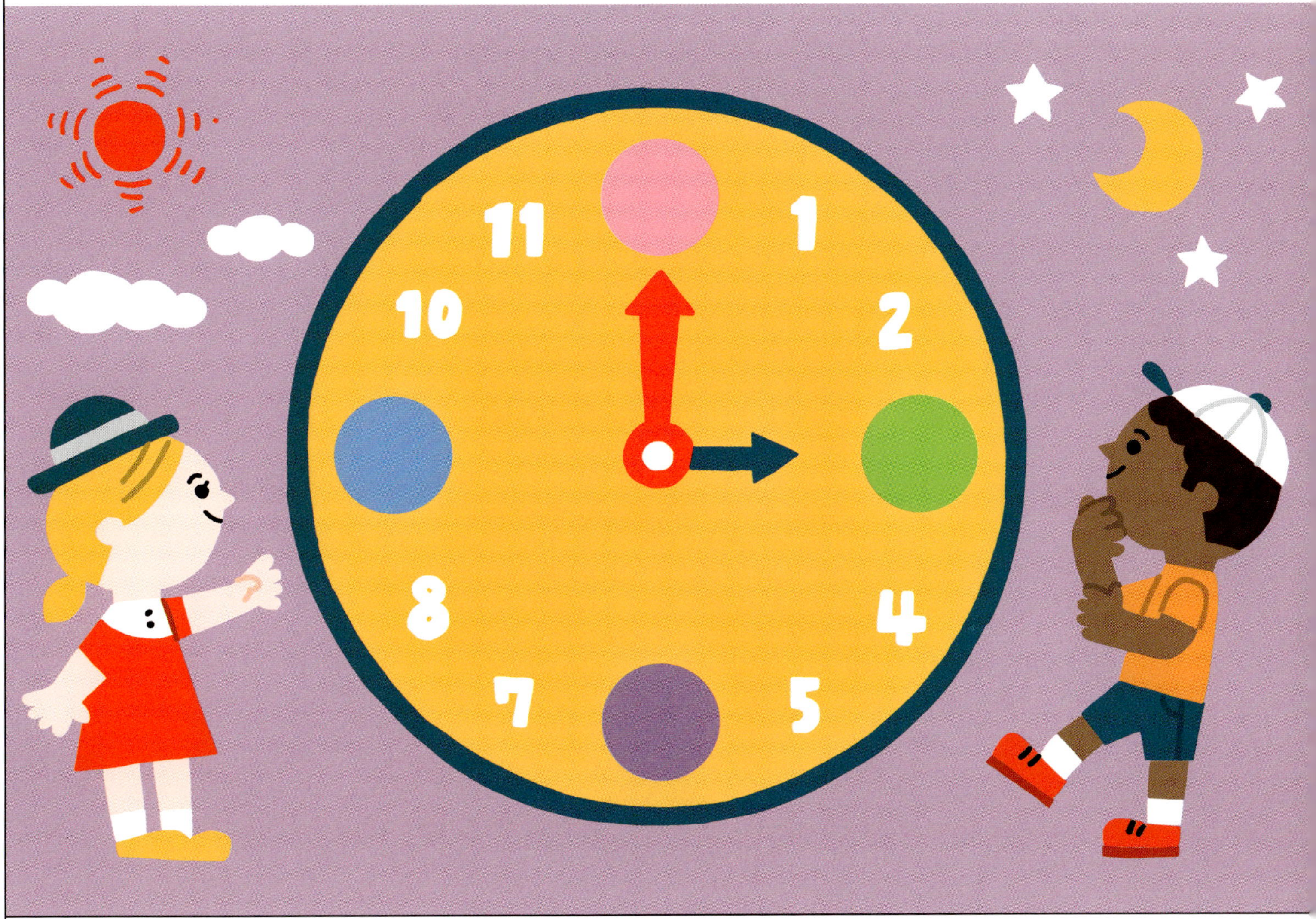

Parents: Please cut along —— for your child.

Parents: Please cut these parts out for your child.

Parents: Please cut along —— for your child.

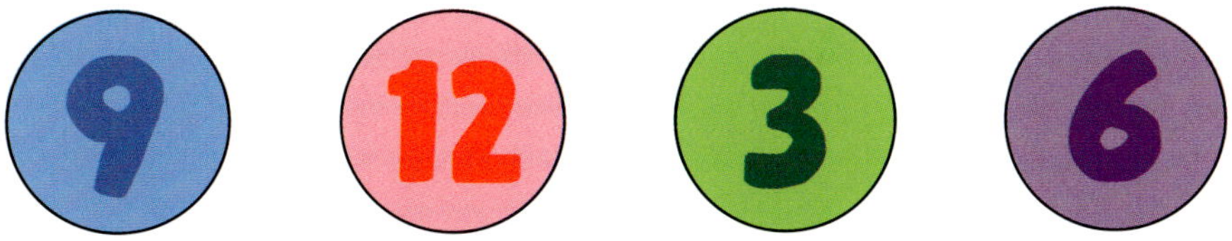

21 Lunchbox

< example >

To parents Your child will paste the food onto the lunchbox. These pieces are equal in size, so your child can paste them wherever he or she likes. When the exercise is finished, ask your child about his or her favorite lunch food.

■ Paste the dishes onto the lunchbox as you like.

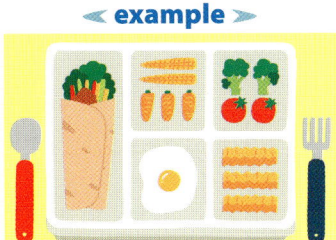

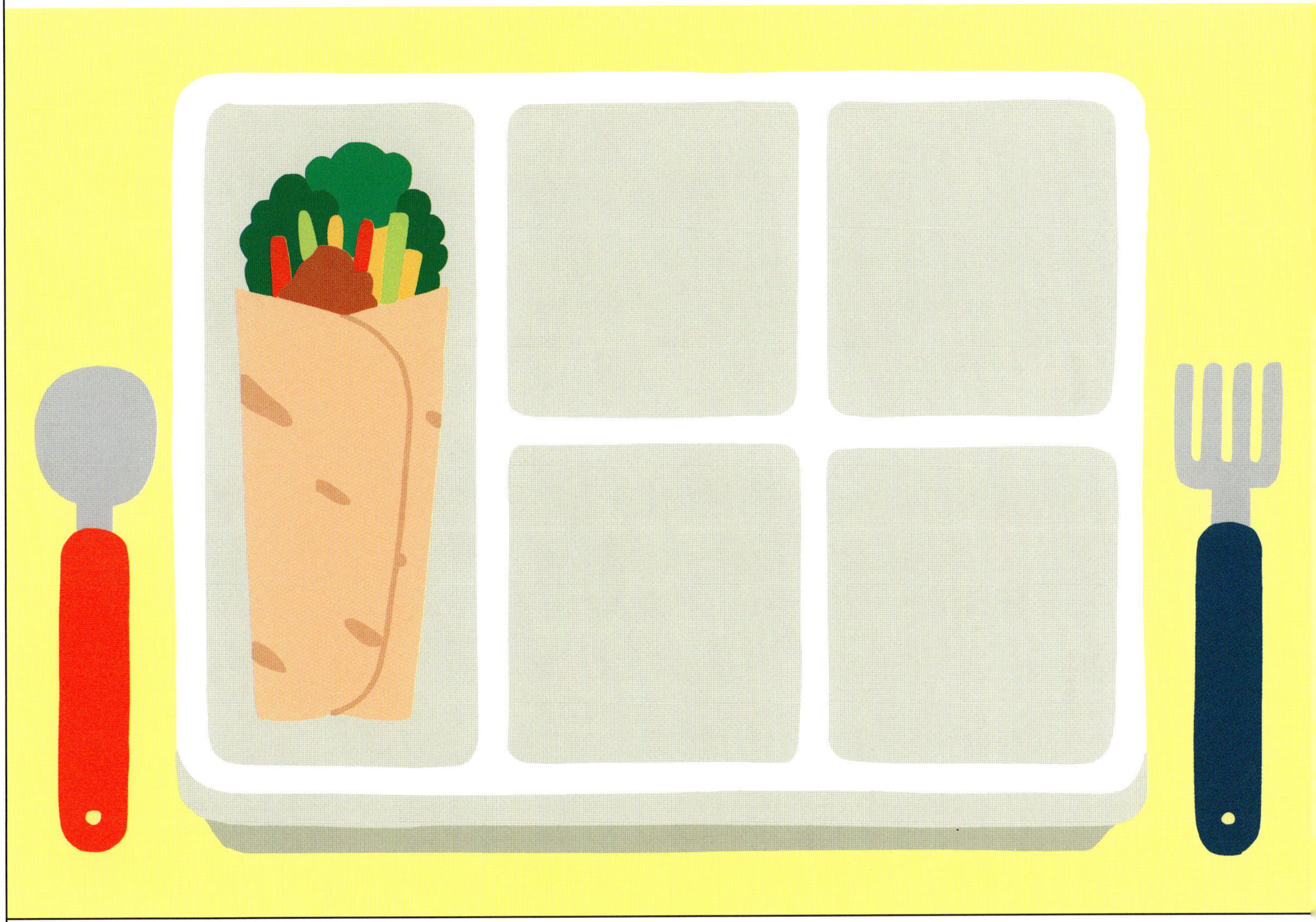

Parents: Please cut along —— for your child.

Parents: Please cut these parts out for your child.

Parents: Please cut along —— for your child.

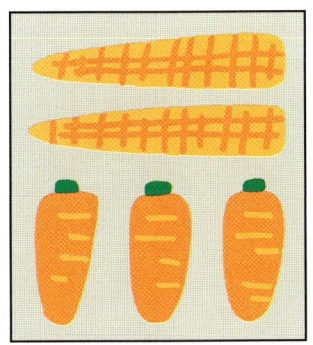

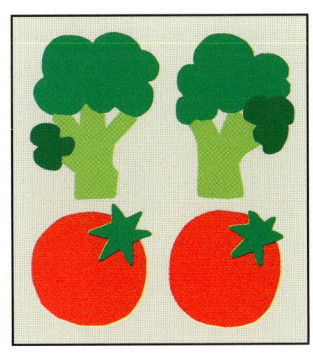

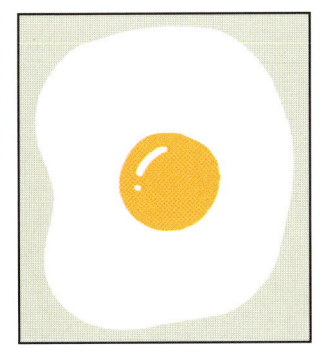

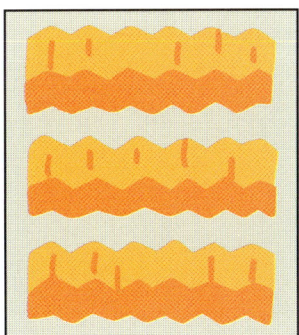

22 Mother's Day

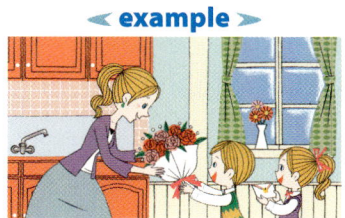

« example »

To parents From this page on, your child will paste the parts as though he or she is completing a puzzle. If your child doesn't know the correct way to paste each part, offer to help. When he or she is finished, offer a lot of praise, such as "Wow! You did a great job!"

■ Paste the cut out parts to complete the picture.

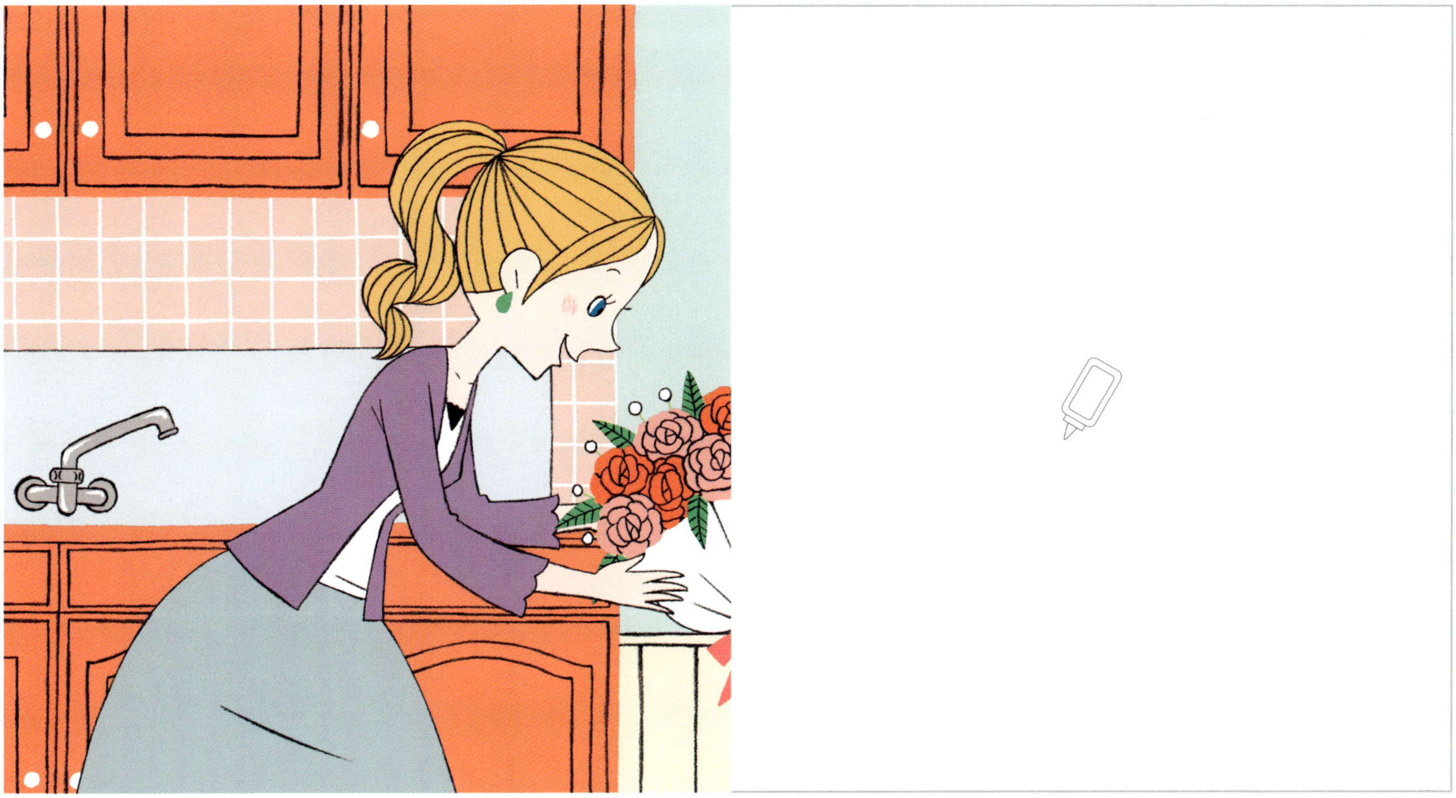

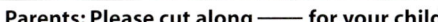

Parents: Please cut along —— for your child.

Parents: Please cut this part out for your child.

Parents: Please cut along —— for your child.

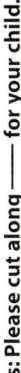

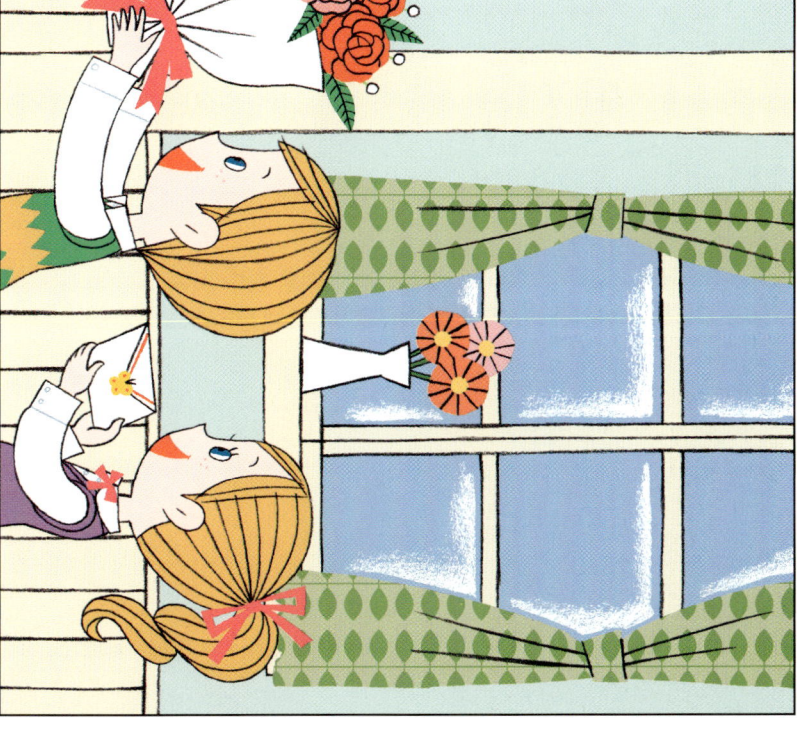

4TH of July

To parents   In this exercise, your child will paste the parts to complete the scene. Encourage your child to try different placements before using glue. When he or she is finished, offer a lot of praise and ask, "Do you like fireworks?"

■ Paste the cut out parts to complete the picture.

Parents: Please cut along ——— for your child.

Parents: Please cut these parts out for your child.

Earth Day

To parents Your child will paste the parts to complete the scene. Encourage your child to pay attention to the orientation and alignment. When he or she is finished, you can talk about how you celebrate Earth Day.

‹ **example** ›

■ Paste the cut out parts to complete the picture.

Parents: Please cut along —— for your child.

Parents: Please cut these parts out for your child.

Parents: Please cut along —— for your child.

To parents Your child should be careful to correctly place and align the parts. If he or she doesn't know the proper position and orientation, please offer to help.

■ Paste the cut out parts to complete the picture.

Parents: Please cut these parts out for your child.

Parents: Please cut along —— for your child.

26 New Year's Eve

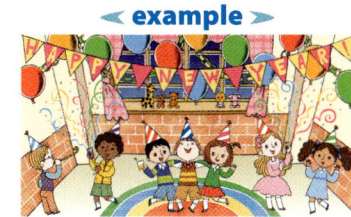

< example >

To parents It is difficult to perfectly align the details of the illustration. So, don't be concerned if the parts are not aligned correctly. Offer your child a lot of praise and say, "New Year's Eve looks like fun!"

■ Paste the cut out parts to complete the picture.

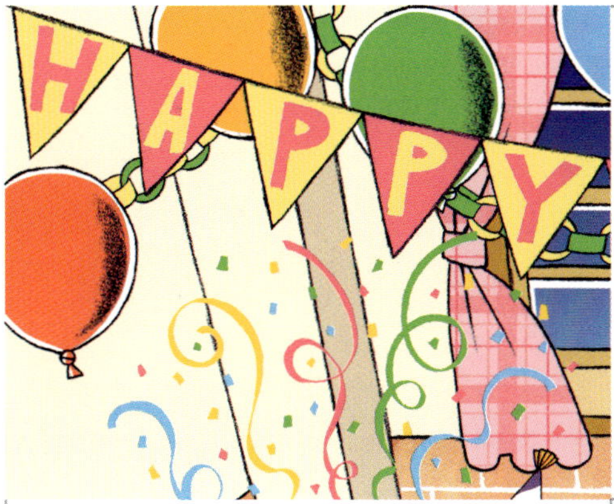

Parents: Please cut along —— for your child.

Parents: Please cut these parts out for your child.

Parents: Please cut along —— for your child.

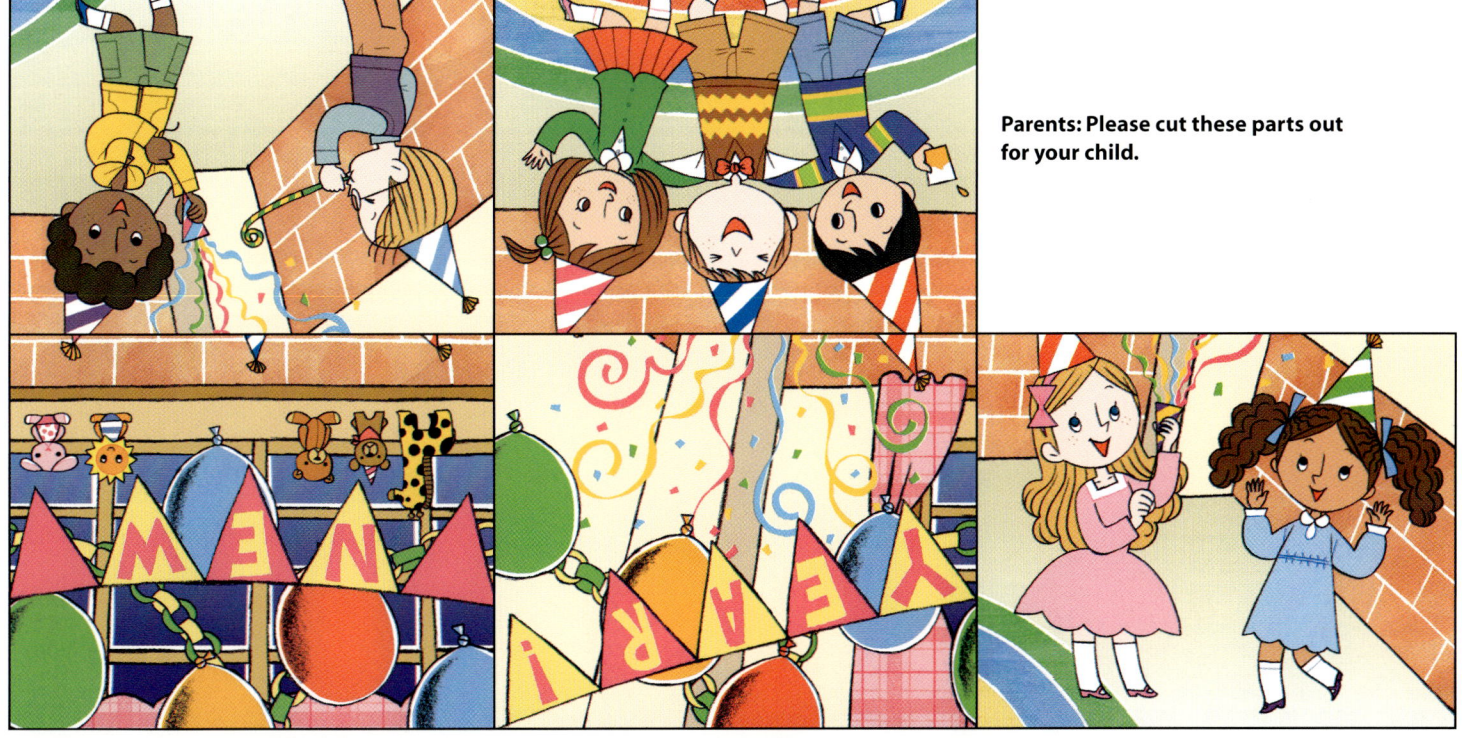

Thanksgiving

‹ **example** ›

To parents   In this exercise, your child will paste all the parts to create the illustration. If your child doesn't know where to place the pieces, offer to help.

■ Paste the cut out parts to complete the picture.

Parents: Please cut these parts out for your child.

Parents: Please cut along —— for your child.

Valentine's Day

< example >

To parents This illustration has a lot of intricate details. If the parts are not perfectly aligned, don't be concerned. When your child is finished, offer a lot of praise.

■ Paste the cut out parts to complete the picture.

Parents: Please cut these parts out for your child.

Parents: Please cut along —— for your child.

Parents: Please cut along —— for your child.

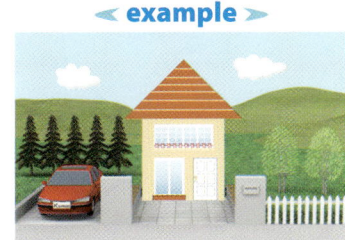

29 Home Sweet Home

To parents Your child will make a picture with these different shapes. Encourage your child to look at the example and paste the pieces according to their shapes.

example

■ Paste the cut out parts to complete the picture.

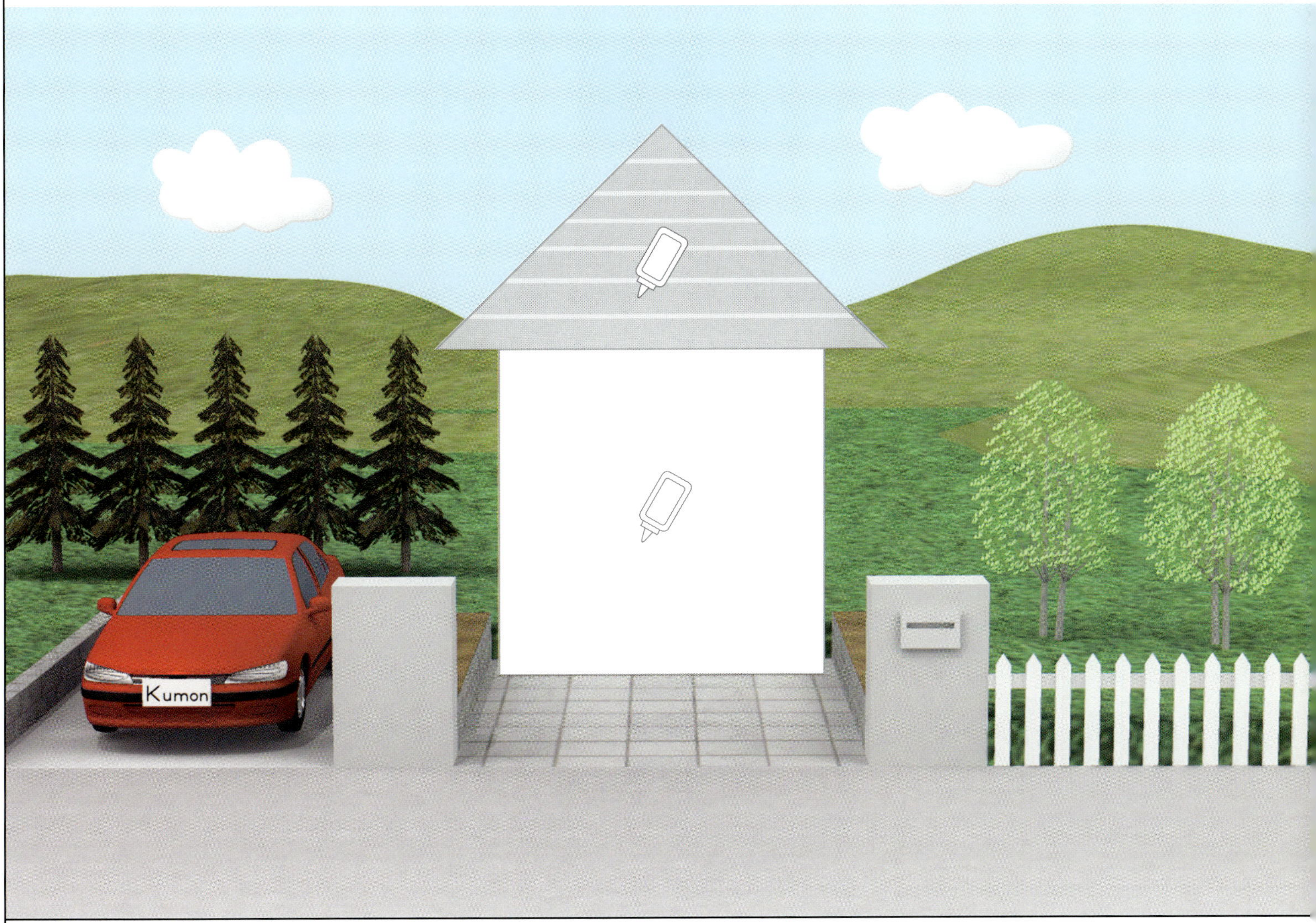

Parents: Please cut along —— for your child.

Parents: Please cut these parts out for your child.

Parents: Please cut along —— for your child.

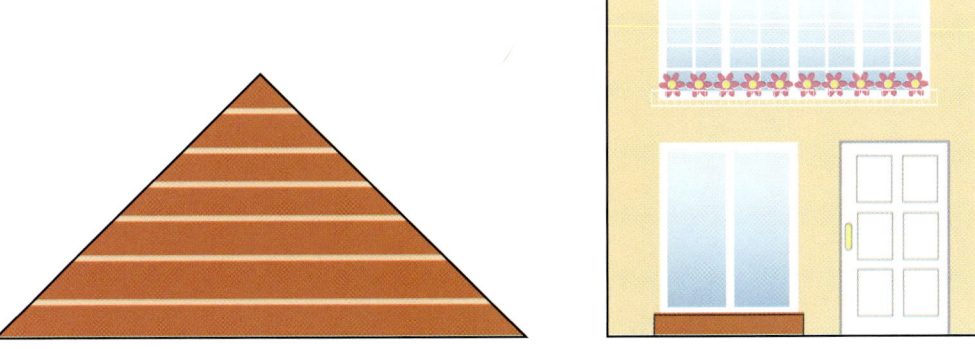

30 Super Express Train

< example >

To parents Your child will make a train with three pieces. If he or she is unsure of where to place each piece, encourage your child to look at the example.

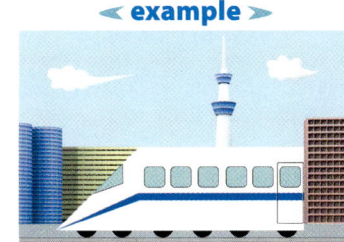

■ Paste the cut out parts to complete the picture.

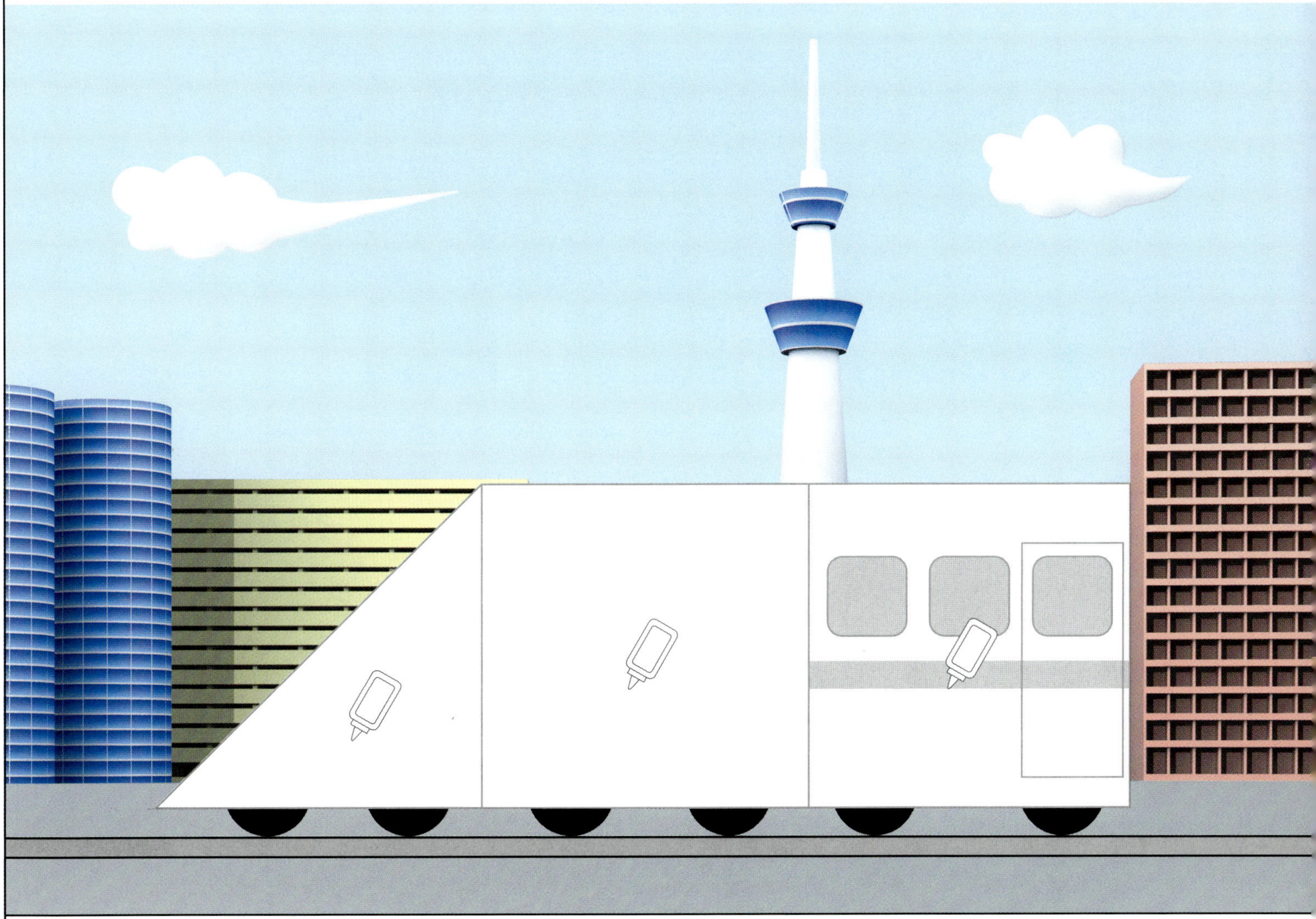

Parents: Please cut along —— for your child.

Parents: Please cut these parts out for your child.

Parents: Please cut along —— for your child.

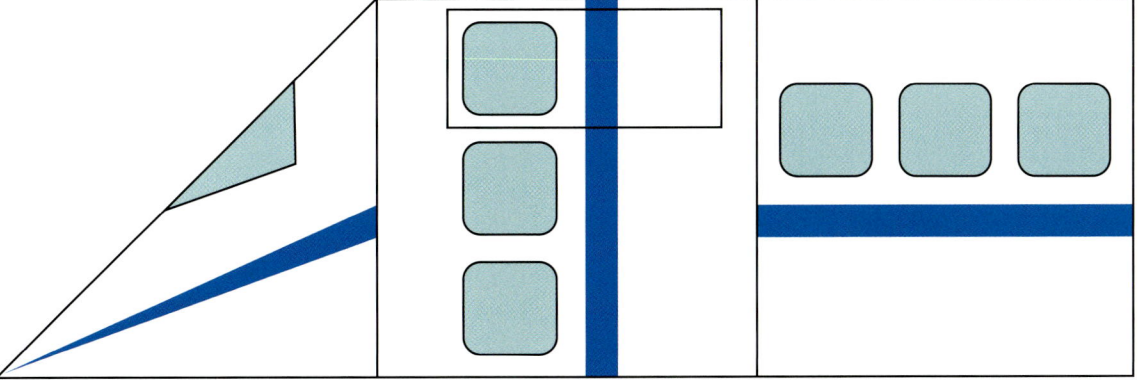

31 Whale

To parents This is the last exercise of the book. When your child is finished, compare this page with his or her previous work. You will see a great deal of progress in your child's ability to accurately paste with glue.

■ Paste the cut out parts to complete the picture.

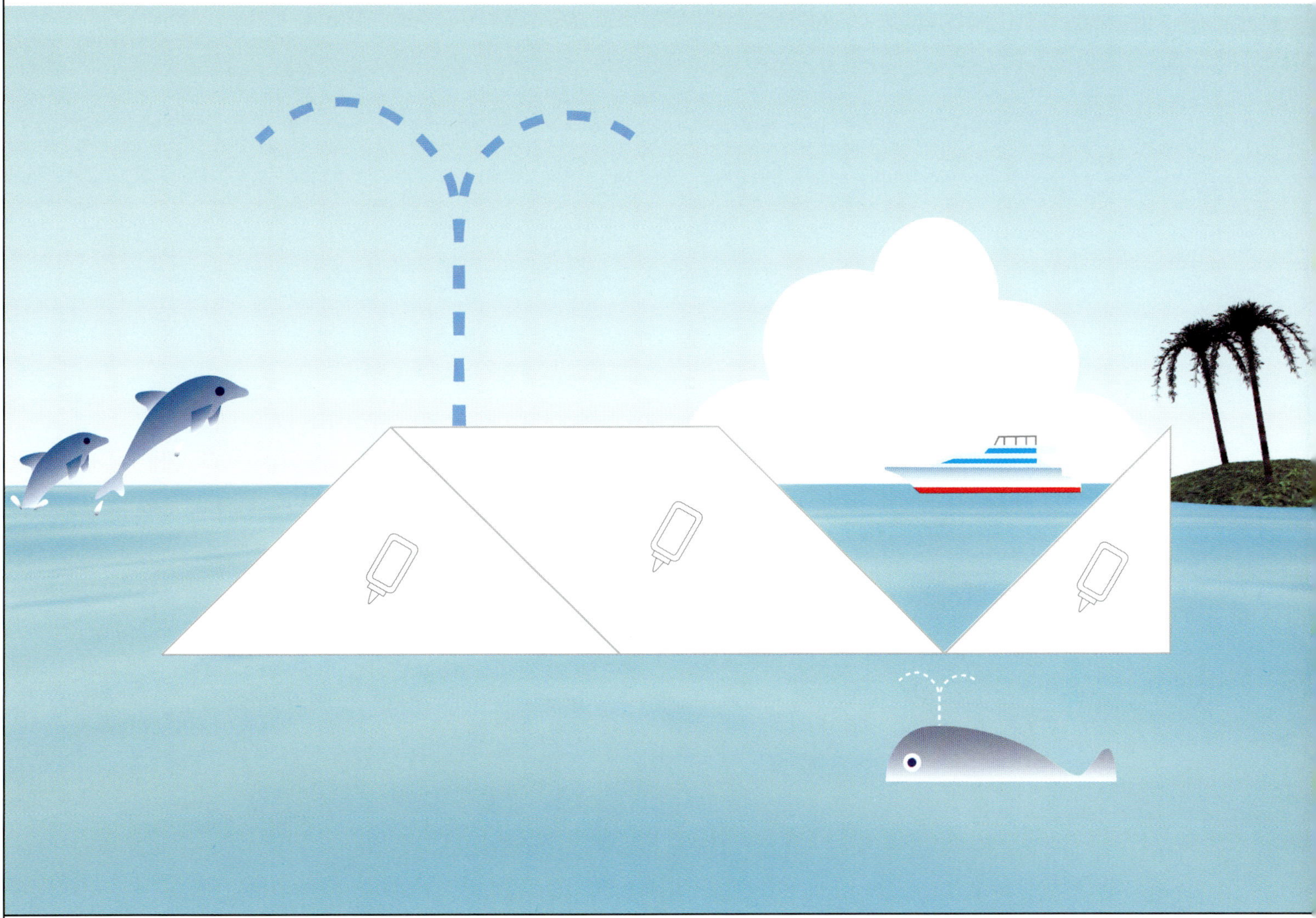

Parents: Please cut along ——— for your child.

Parents: Please cut along ——— for your child.

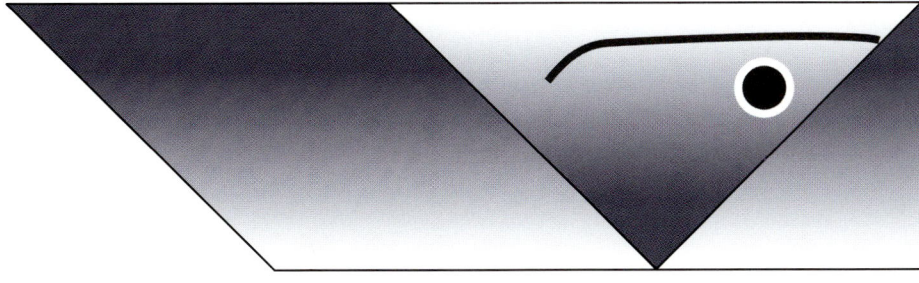

Parents: Please cut these parts out for your child.

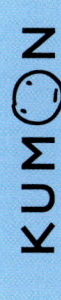

KUM☺N

Certificate of Achievement

is hereby congratulated on completing

Are You Ready for Kindergarten? Pasting Skills

Presented on _____ , 20 _____

_____
Parent or Guardian